GIFT KNITS

GIFT KNITS

More Than 70 Wearable & Decorative Projects

Chris Rankin

A Sterling/Lark Book

Sterling Publishing Co., Inc.   New York

Editor: Dawn Cusick
Art Director: Sandra Montgomery
Production: Elaine Thompson, Sandra Montgomery
English Translation: Networks, Inc.

Library of Congress Cataloging-in-Publication Data
Rankin, Chris.
    Gift knits : more than 70 wearable & decorative projects / [Chris Rankin].
      p.   cm.
    "A Sterling/Lark book."
    Includes bibliographical references and index.
    ISBN 0-8069-8842-8
    1. Knitting—Patterns. I. Title
TT820.R337   1993
746.43'2—dc20   92–37393
                                                         CIP

10 9 8 7 6 5 4 3 2 1

A Sterling/Lark Book

Produced by Altamont Press, Inc.
50 College St., Asheville, NC 28801

Published in 1993 by Sterling Publishing Co., Inc.
387 Park Ave. S., New York, NY 10016

Photos and instructions © Ariadne/Spaarnestad, Utrecht, Holland
English Translation © 1993, Altamont Press

Distributed in Canada by Sterling Publishing,
c/o Canadian Manda Group, P.O. Box 920, Station U, Toronto,
        Ontario M8Z 5P9
Distributed in the United Kingdom by Cassell PLC, Villiers House,
        41/47 Strand, London WC2N 5JE, England
Distributed in Australia by Capricorn Link, Ltd., P.O. Box 665,
        Lane Cove, NSW 2066

Every effort has been made to ensure that all information in this book is
accurate. However, due to differing conditions, tools, and individual skills,
the publisher cannot be responsible for any injuries, losses, or other damages
which may result from the use of the information in this book.

Printed in Hong Kong

ISBN 0-8069-8842-8

Table of Contents

Introduction

The frustration...ah, the frustration. Everyone who loves to knit knows the feeling. You want to share your craft with the special people in your life — not to mention use up all those balls of yarn leftover from previous projects — but there just aren't many options. Yes, you can make them a sweater, but that's a large investment of time and money for something you can't be sure will be appreciated…not to mention the difficulties of making sure a surprise sweater will fit well. In Gift Knits, you'll find projects that take up just the right amount of time and yarn. There are projects for everyone on your list…plus lots of special projects to make for yourself.

Celebrate birthdays and Christmas for the children in your life with pullovers decorated with colorful motifs including sheriffs, snowflakes, goldfish, polar bears, trucks, and even Santa Claus; or, if you'd like to make something smaller, you'll find mittens, hast, sweater and bootie sets, toys and dolls, leg warmers, and even a bikini. To welcome a new baby, you'll find blankets, bottle warmers, bibs, and pullovers.

For the grown-up kids there are bow ties, neck ties, bracelets, gloves, mitten and scarf sets, socks, pullovers, collectible dolls, plus much more. To decorate the home there are pot holders, holiday tree ornaments, kitchen towels, cooking mitts, and sachets. Now your only frustration will be in finding time to make all of these exciting projects!

Knit One, Purl One

▼ Success Tips

The majority of the projects in this book use simple knitting techniques, and you shouldn't have trouble following the pattern directions. Since most of the projects are worked in more than one color, though, you may need to review the following instructions and illustrations before you try your first multi-colored project. Remember to make a test swatch to check the gauge before you begin a project (even if you're using the same size needles and yarn called for in the directions), and to keep your sense of humor as you continue making additional swatches until you get the correct gauge. This book uses standard knitting abbreviations, which you can study in the chart below if you're unfamiliar with them. Beginning knitters can refer to the basic knitting instructions in one of the many how-to books on the market.

Abbreviations

inc = decrease
dec = decrease
St st = Stockinette stitch
beg = begin(ning)
foll = follow(ing)
pat = pattern
sts = stitches
MC = main color
CC = contrasting color
tog = together

Knitting with More than One Color

Most knitters are surprised to discover that knitting with two or more colors is easier than it looks. It can be done with a single technique or by combining several different techniques. European knitters often refer to color change techniques as "jacquard knitting," in honor of the French inventor, J.M. Jacquard, who developed a knitting machine with punch cards that could change colors.

Included under the generic heading of jacquard knitting is intarsia knitting, fairisle knitting, and many combinations of the two. The basic difference between these two techniques hinges on whether the unused yarn is carried across the wrong side on the stitches in another color (fairisle), or whether the two colors are crossed at their juncture (intarsia).

Most color knitting and embroidery is done on a flat stitch surface, usually the stockinette stitch. Stockinette stitch is knit on the right side and purled on the wrong side. Most of the projects in this book are worked exclusively in the stockinette stitch, though some patterns also use the reverse stockinette stitch to form ridges, relief stripes, or patterns. Reverse stockinette stitch is purled on the right side and knit on the wrong side. Most sweaters are designed using a 1/1 or 2/2 ribbing for the borders. To work a ribbing, alternately knit and purl every stitch (1/1) or every two stitches (2/2) and knit each following row as established.

Fairisle Knitting

True fairisle knitting is always done in the round, but the term is commonly used to refer to any stranded color change technique. A stranded technique requires the use of more than one color in a row. Stitches in one color are knit, then a new color is introduced. The yarn color not being used is loosely carried across the wrong side of the work. A chart is used to determine which color is used for which stitches.

The hardest part of fairisle knitting is maintaining the proper tension when changing colors. The easiest way to do that is to continually spread out the stitches of the color just knit so that you have allowed enough yarn to stretch across the wrong side of the work without pulling. After you have completed one color, drop it, pick up the next color, and continue knitting. Take care not to cross the new color of yarn with the yarn just knit; instead just lay it next to the previous color. For example, if you were knitting in red and blue, you would try to always lay the red yarn over the blue or vice versa. If you do cross the yarns, they will become very tangled. One of the advantages of machine knitting intarsia designs is that the carriage maintains an even tension on the strands on the wrong side of the work. However, these strands may be very long and, unlike hand knitting, will not be woven in. Take care to select a pattern with no more than four or five stitches between colors.

One of the "rules" of fairisle knitting is to never use more than two colors in a row. This rule can

Fairisle Knitting

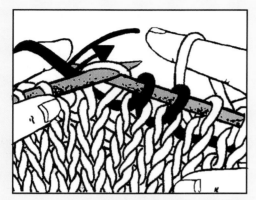

▼*Knitting with right hand, stranding with left*

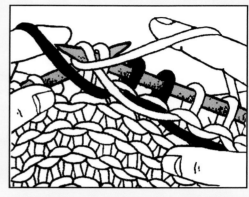

▼*Purling with right hand, stranding with left*

▼*Knitting with left hand, stranding with right*

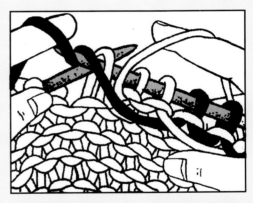

▼*Purling with left hand, stranding with right*

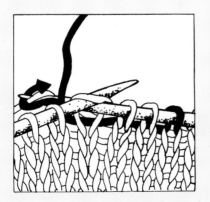

▼*Crossing yarns when changing colors on knit rows*

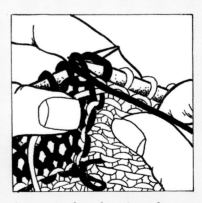

▼*Crossing yarns when changing colors on purl rows*

be violated, but it is hard to maintain the correct tension, and the knitting becomes extremely bulky when too many strands are carried across the wrong side of the work. If you are working with a fine yarn, however, bulk may not be a drawback. Remember also that if you want to use more than two colors in a row, you can use duplicate stitch embroidery to add a color over a stitch. Since you can introduce two new colors in every row, the number of colors used in a sweater is practically limitless.

Another "rule" is to never knit more than four or five neighboring stitches in one color because it is too difficult to maintain the proper tension on the carried yarn. Tension can be maintained by weaving in the carried yarn. Simply hold it flat against the back of the work and use the running strand you are knitting with to catch the unused color. Check the work periodically because a highly contrasting color may show through the front of the work. You must be very careful about your tension so the stitches don't appear pulled. At the end of the row, the yarn should be carried along the seam edges, allowing enough give in the yarn so it doesn't pull up the rows.

In most cases the fairisle technique is worked in stockinette stitch (knit right side of work rows, purl wrong side of work rows) because the smooth background is an ideal backdrop for color. When you alternately knit and purl stitches, the yarn change from the previous row will show—half of the stitch will be in one color and half in the second color. To avoid this, always work the first row of the new color in the stockinette stitch.

Many of these patterns use a striped ribbing. To create a smooth transition from one color to another, knit the first row of a new color on the right side of the work. The ribbing of the previous and following rows will make this row look like ribbing.

Sometimes you may want to use a color for only one row. The result of this is that the ball of the completed color will hang at the opposite end of the row from where you began. If you work back and forth on a double pointed circular needle, you can begin knitting at either end, wherever the color you want is hanging. This prevents a lot of cutting and tying on of colors and amazingly doesn't alter the appearance of the finished work. Just be sure to always knit the right side of work rows and purl the wrong side for the stockinette stitch.

Intarsia Knitting

Intarsia knitting is like painting with yarn. Each section of color is considered separate from the surrounding color. Usually the different colored sections of the designs are larger than a few stitches and may continue vertically or diagonally across the knitting, while a fairisle design is primarily horizontal. The back side of intarsia knitting is neat and unstranded and the bulk is much less than a similar fairisle design. Machine knitting intarsia requires the use of an intarsia carriage and much hand work of laying yarn across the needles, but it is still faster than hand knitting.

The main difficulty with intarsia knitting is keeping the different color yarns from becoming tangled. Often bobbins are used

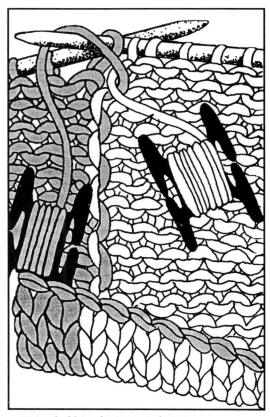
▼*Using bobbins for intarsia knitting*

because they allow only short lengths of yarn to be free. If you are working with many colors at a time, you can leave long strands of each color hanging loose, unballed or bobbined. Since there is no obstruction at the end, the strands can be untangled relatively easily. Don't try this with mohair or other yarns which like to cuddle up with each other or you will spend more time untangling than knitting. Some inventions developed to deal with this problem include boxes with separate compartments for each ball of yarn. You can also put each ball of yarn in a plastic bag with a wire tie to keep it closed.

Then the yarn can only tangle with the length that's not in the bag. To keep the yarn from tangling at the end of rows, be systematic: turn to the left at the end of purl rows, turn to the right for knit rows.

Often intarsia knitting becomes fairisle knitting when the same color is used for two motifs near each other. Rather than using a separate ball for each section, you may want to carry the strand across the connecting stitches. In that case, you must use care to maintain the proper tension on the unused yarn just as in fairisle knitting.

Adding Colors without Knitting

If you're new to multi-color knitting and still feel intimidated, (or if you just don't have the patience for all those extra lengths of yarn) you may want to add additional colors by using embroidery stitches or vertical stripes with a crochet hook. Even if you feel totally comfortable with fairisle and intarsia knitting, there are still times when embroidering the color just makes more sense, such as when you only need to add two Xs for sheep eyes.

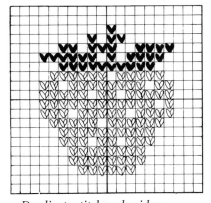

▼*Duplicate stitch embroidery*

The most common embroidery done on knitting is duplicate stitch, also called Swiss darning, although cross stitch will also work as long as you're careful to avoid stretching the knitted fabric. Duplicate stitch embroidery duplicates the stitch of the knitting by covering up the original stitch. It can be worked with the same kind of yarn as the original knitting or with cotton embroidery floss or tapestry wool. In many cases, especially when you're working with a highly contrasting color or yarn of a different weight, parts of the original stitch will show through, although this often creates natural-looking shadows in the motif's outlines.

Duplicate stitch embroidery is usually done with a blunt-tip, large-

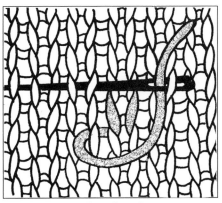

▼*Duplicate stitch embroidery*

eyed needle, usually called a yarn or tapestry needle. First insert the threaded needle from the wrong side to the right side at the base of the stitch. Next, insert the needle under the two strands of the base of the stitch above and pull through; then insert the needle at the same point as the entry. Adjust the tension on the thread to cover the stitch below. If you'll be working a lot of stitches in a row, it's best to

work across the row, then move up one stitch and work in the opposite direction across the row above. Sometimes it's easier to work vertically rather than horizontally, but it really doesn't matter as long as you check the back of the work frequently for neatness. (The more times you carry strands of yarn over many stitches to get to the next section, the messier the back will look.) This is especially important in garments such as cardigans where the inside may be visible.

To add color with cross stitch, work from the back to the front and insert the needle between two stitches under the strand connecting the two stitches. Then cross the stitch diagonally to the right and insert the needle behind the strand between stitches. Cross the same stitch diagonally to the left and insert the needle behind the strand between stitches. Continue in the same way.

The following embroidery stitch descriptions and illustrations can be used as inspiration for adding

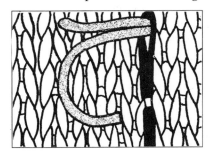

▼*Cross Stitch*

designs with color. The stitches can be worked freehand, without reference to the original knitted

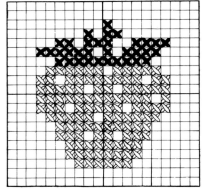

▼*Cross stitch embroidery*

stitches if you feel comfortable working that way, or the design can be reproduced with an enlarging copy machine and then transferred to the knitted fabric by outlining the design with basting thread.

Chain stitch: This stitch is used to make lines such as stems or to make petals on daisies and other flowers. Working from back to front, come up at a point and reinsert the needle at the same point, making a loop. With your finger, hold the top of the loop against the work at the desired point. Reinsert the needle inside the loop and make a small stitch to hold the top of the loop. To make a line, reinsert the needle at the top of the loop and begin the next chain. To make flower petals, work single loops as indicated on a chart.

Stem stitch: The stem stitch is used, surprisingly, to make stems or other lines which can easily turn direction or form curves. Working from back to front, come up at one point, go to wrong side a short distance later. Bring the needle to

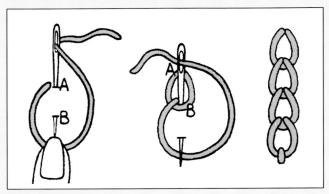

▼*Chain stitch*

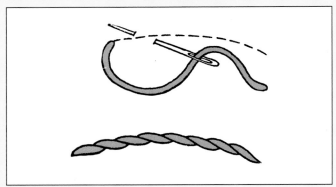

▼*Stem stitch*

▼*Outline stitch*

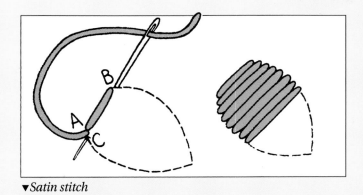

▼*Satin stitch*

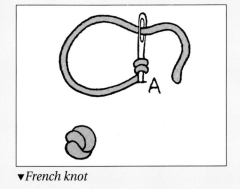

▼*French knot*

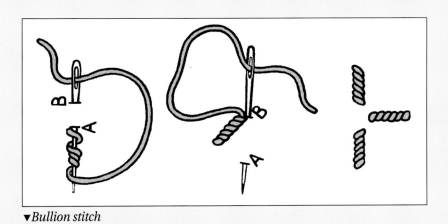

▼*Bullion stitch*

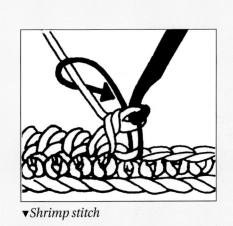

▼*Shrimp stitch*

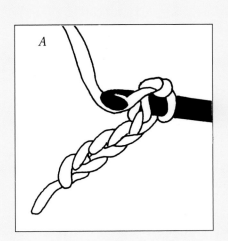

A

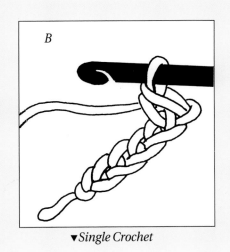

B

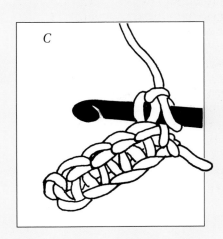

C

▼*Single Crochet*

the front halfway on the first stitch. Insert the needle the same distance as the previous stitch and continue as before.

Outline stitch: The outline stitch is used to surround embroidered areas or to make lines as part of a motif. It is also called a back stitch when one stitch follows another. It is the easiest stitch to make. Working from back to front, come up at one point, and go down to the wrong side a short distance later.

Satin stitch: The satin stitch is used to fill in an area of a motif. It is easiest to work from the widest section and work to the narrowest section. The satin stitch is a combination of many outline stitches. Working from back to front, come up at one point, go down to the wrong side at the designated point. As close as possible to the original insertion point, come up again and repeat until the entire area is filled in.

French knot: French knots are used as the centers of flowers, as buds, or wherever a raised spot of color is required. Working from back to front, come up at one point, twist yarn around needle once and reinsert needle at the same point.

Bullion stitch: The bullion stitch is like a long French knot. Working from back to front, insert needle at beginning of line to be covered and reinsert at the end of the line, leaving a loop. Reinsert the needle at the beginning point and twist around the loop of yarn, pull the needle through the twists and insert the needle at the point where the twisted yarn will lie flat against the fabric.

Crocheted stripes

Crocheted chain stitch stripes are worked on knit fabrics because they are so much easier to add to finished knitting than to knit in stripes as single stitches. When worked over a flat surface, they also give a raised effect on the surface, or can blend in when reverse stockinette vertical stripes are knit into a design. The crocheted stripes then are worked over the purl stitches, bringing them up to the level of the knitted stitches.

Hold the yarn on the wrong side of the work and insert the crochet hook to wrong side of work. Pull up a loop of yarn. Reinsert the hook one row above the original point and pull up another loop. Draw the second loop through the first and continue in this way. Unless a pattern indicates otherwise, each crocheted loop should be one row long.

Crocheting may also be used to make simple edgings on necks or front edges in single crochet or shrimp stitch.

Single crochet (sc): Insert hook into the second chain from the hook. Wrap the yarn around the hook from back to front. Draw the yarn through the chain making 2 loops on the hook. Wrap yarn around hook and pull through 2 loops on hook. One single crochet stitch has been completed. Continue by inserting the hook in the next chain. After the last stitch, chain 2 and turn; insert the hook into the first stitch to begin the next row.

Shrimp stitch: Worked like single crochet, but worked in the opposite direction, that is, left to right, instead of right to left. Keep the right side of the work facing you as you work.

Color Charts

Most projects with more than one color will have a chart to show color changes. The charts are read from the lower right corner to the left, unless otherwise specified. In some cases, an arrow is used to indicate where to begin or where to center a chart. To determine where to start a row when you only know the center stitch, mark the center stitch of your knitting and count back to the beginning of the row. Count from the center of the chart on row 1 to the beginning of row one. When you have the same number of stitches on the chart as on your knitting, begin there. If you don't have enough stitches on the chart to cover your actual stitches, resume counting from the left end of row 1 toward the right end. For example, if your chart

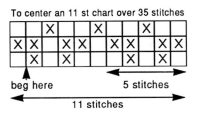

To center an 11 st chart over 35 stitches

beg here   5 stitches

11 stitches

has 11 stitches and the 6th stitch is marked as the center and you have 35 stitches on your needle, you will have 17 stitches at each side of the center stitch. You will have 5 stitches at the right of the center stitch; begin counting again from the left end of the chart. After one full repeat, return to the left edge of the chart and count back one stitch. This equals 17 stitches. Begin your knitting at this point. Often the beginning stitch for the different sizes will be indicated on the chart. You may be asked to repeat between one point and another on a chart a certain number of times and then between two other points to finish the row. If you read carefully, this is easy to do.

You may or may not be required to work a border stitch at each edge of the chart. A border stitch is usually knit in stockinette stitch to make it easy to sew into a seam. It is usually knit in the background color or in the same color as the adjacent stitch. Since it will only be part of the seam allowance, its color doesn't matter. The main function of border stitches is to prevent any part of a motif from disappearing into a seam.

Since a chart represents a certain number of stitches and rows, it is crucial that you get the stitch and row gauge given in the pattern or the chart will not fit and the proportion of the motif may significantly change. In some kinds of knitting, row gauge may not be very significant, since we usually consider size a function of width. In these cases, length can easily be adjusted by adding or subtracting rows, but in any kind of color change pattern, the difference of a few rows is very significant.

If your gauge is 20 stitches x 30 rows in 4 inches, each stitch is one-third wider than it is long. If you want to form a square, you have to knit a multiple of 2 stitches and 3 rows. If you have a gauge of 20 stitches x 25 rows in 4 inches and want to form a square, you would have to use a multiple of 2 stitches and 2-1/2 rows. If you followed a chart for the first gauge on a piece knitted to the second gauge, your designs would be elongated. Keep this in mind if you cannot get the gauge called for in the pattern and have to make adjustments as you go. This is much easier if you're embroidering on the colors because you can just pull out a few stitches if they don't look right as opposed to unraveling a few dozen rows of knitting if you notice that something looks funny after you've completed a large motif.

Around the Home

Colorful Pot Holders

▼ Materials

Cotton fabric; U.S. size 15 (10 mm) knitting needles, U.S. size J/10 (6 mm) crochet hook

▼ Gauge

U.S. size 15 (10 mm) needles in garter st: 4" = 10 sts x 18 rows.

To save time, take time to check gauge!

▼ Directions

Cut fabric into 1/4" (1 cm) wide strips. Sew the ends to make long strands and wind into a ball. Cast on 13 sts and work 5-1/4" (15 cm) in garter st. Bind off. Work 1 round of sc around pot holder as foll: 1 sc in each st and 2 sc in each corner. On one end, ch 7 and sl st to last sc to form loop. Fasten off.

Christmas Tree Angels

▼ Materials

Fingering weight mercerized yarn in White and Pink, embroidery floss in Orange, Pink and Turquoise, 3 wooden rings with an inner diameter of 2" (5 cm), stuffing, 3 wooden beads 3/4" (2 cm) wide, turquoise and white paint, colored cord, thin white double strand canvas, hobby glue, tracing paper, spray varnish; U.S. size 2 (2.5 mm) knitting needles, U.S. size B/1 (2 mm) crochet hook

▼ Directions

ANGEL WITH BALL

BODY: With white, cast on 40 sts and work in St st. Rows 1 to 6: St st (first row on the right side of work). Row 7: *K2, k2 tog*, rep * to * = 30 sts. Rows 8 to 20: St st. Row 21: *K1, k2 tog*, rep * to * = 20 sts = neck. Continue in pink for head. Row 1: (wrong side of work): *P2, p2 in the foll st*, rep * to *, end with p2 = 26 sts. Rows 2 to 11: St st. Row 12: *K3, k2 tog*, rep * to *, end with k1 = 21 sts. Row 13: Purl. Row 14: *K2, k2 tog*, rep * to *, end with k1 = 16 sts. Row 15:

Purl. Row 16: *K1, k2 tog*, rep * to *, end with k1 = 11 sts. Place sts on holder.

ARMS: With white, cast on 12 sts and work in St st for 7 rows. Row 8: K2 tog across row = 6 sts. Rows 9 to 13: With pink, work in St st, then place sts on holder.

FINISHING: Fold the body in half right sides tog. Sew lengthwise seam and place seam at center of back. Sew the lower edge and turn right side out and stuff. Gather yarn at top of body and fasten off. Gather at neck. Fold the arms in half right sides tog. Turn right side out. Gather top of arms, stuff arms and sew to body. Embroider the mouth in pink over the center st of the pink row above the neck. Work 2 sts in orange for the cheeks and embroider eyes in turquoise on the 8th row in pink. Cut 45 strands of white yarn 4" (10 cm) long and sew to center of the head. Glue down the underhairs. Trim hair and bangs. Make a pattern for wings on tracing paper and cut out of canvas. Make sharp fold in center of canvas and sew to back of angel. Paint a bead turquoise with white dots and spray varnish and glue between hands. Make a chain with turquoise embroidery floss 4-1/4" (11 cm) long. Fasten off and sew to crown of angel's head.

RING ANGEL

BODY: With white, cast on 30 sts and work in St st. Rows 1 to 10: St st. Row 11: *K1, k2 tog*, rep * to * = 20 sts. Row 12: With pink, continue for head and

arms as on other angel.

FINISHING: Work same as angel with ball, but sew the hands tog. Paint the ring turquoise, then paint white dots. Make a chain as above and wrap around ring. Glue angel to ring.

Pattern for Wings

Country Pot Holders and Towel

▼ Materials

Mayflower Helarsgarn (50 g) 1 ball
Yellow for pot holder, 2 balls Yellow for
towel; U.S. size 4 (3.5 mm) knitting
needles, U.S. size D/3 (3.5mm) crochet
hook

▼ Gauge

U.S. size 4 (3.5 mm) needles in pat st
foll chart: 4" (10 cm) = 20 sts x 29 rows.

To save time, take time to check gauge!

▼ Directions

POT HOLDER

Cast on 34 sts. Rows 1 to 5: Knit. Row 6:
K3, p28, k3. Continue by foll chart beg
with row 1. When chart is complete,
knit last row (wrong side) as you bind
off.

TOWEL

Cast on 86 sts and work as foll: Rows 1
to 5: Knit. Row 6: K3, p80, k3. Row 7:
Knit. Row 8: K3, *p2, k11*, rep * to * 6
times, p2, k3. Continue by foll chart,
beg with row 1. When piece is 6 blocks
wide and 3 blocks high, work last 4
rows of chart twice. Knit last row as you
bind off.

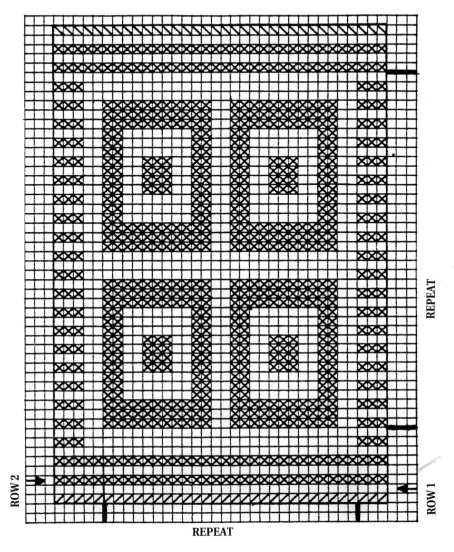

CHART for Pot Holder and Towel

KEY TO CHART

⊠ = P1 on right side,
k1 on wrong side

□ = K1 on right side,
p1 on wrong side

⟋ = Cast on ridge

⟍ = Bind off ridge

Snowflake Pot Holders & Mitts

FINISHED MEASUREMENTS

Dish Towel
20-3/4" x 20-1/2" - (53 x 52 cm)

Potholder
8-1/4" x 8-1/4" - (21 x 21 cm)

Mitt
11-3/4" (30 cm)

▼ Materials

Mayflower Helarsgarn (50 g) 4 balls Red, 4 balls White; U.S. size 4 (3.5 mm) knitting needles, double pointed needles U.S. size 4 (3 mm); red and white dish cloth

▼ Gauge

U.S. size 4 (3.5 mm) needles in St st: 4" (10 cm) = 20 sts x 21 rows.

To save time, take time to check gauge!

▼ Directions

DISHCLOTH

With red, cast on 107 sts and work as foll: Row 1: Purl. Rows 2 and 3: Work in St st. Rows 4-9: 1 border st, 2 sts in red, 101 sts in diagonal stripe pattern foll chart 2, 2 sts in red, 1 border st. Carry unused color loosely across wrong side of work. Rows 10-52: 1 border st, 2 sts in red, 5 sts in diagonal stripe pat, 43 sts of star motif foll chart 1, 5 sts in diagonal stripe pat, 43 st foll chart 1, 5 sts in diagonal stripe st, 2 sts in red, 1 border st. Rows 53-58: Like rows 4-9. Rows 59-101: Like rows 10-52. Rows 102-107: Like rows 4-9. Rows 108-110: St st in red. Bind off.

POT HOLDER

With red, cast on 43 sts and work as foll: Row 1: Purl. Rows 2-3: Work in St st. Rows 4-7: 1 border st, 2 sts in red, work foll 37 sts in diagonal stripe pat foll chart 2, 2 sts in red, 1 border st. Rows 8-38: 1 border st, 2 sts in red, 3 sts in diagonal stripe pat, work 31 sts foll star motif foll chart 3, 3 sts in diagonal stripe pat, 2 sts in red, 1 border st. Rows 39-42: Like rows 4-7. Rows 43-45: Work in St st in red. Bind off in red. Make a 2nd pot holder.

RIGHT MITT

With double pointed needles and red, cast on 60 sts and work 4 rounds in St

st, marking the beg of round. Rounds 1-3: Work in St st in red. Rounds 4-9: Work in diagonal stripe pat foll chart 2. Round 10: St st in red. Round 11: Work 30 sts in fairisle pat foll chart 4. For the thumb foll chart 5 (= inc 1 st in the strand between sts, k1, inc 1 st in the strand between sts, work in diagonal stripe pattern foll chart 6 = 62 sts. Rounds 12-32: Work 30 sts foll chart 4, work thumb sts foll chart 5, work 29 sts for diagonal stripe patterns foll chart 6. After the 32nd round = 82 sts. Round 33: Work 30 sts foll chart 4, place 23 sts for thumb on a holder, cast on 1 st in red, 29 sts in diagonal stripe pat. Work over 60 sts foll charts 4 and 6 until piece is 5-1/2" (14 cm) measured from beg. Shape top: With red, k1, sl 1, k1, psso, 25 sts in pat st, with red, k2 tog, k1, sl 1, k1, psso, 25 sts in diagonal

stripe pat, k2 tog with red. Rep dec once every 2nd round and every round 11 times. Break yarn and thread through rem 8 sts. Pick up 23 sts for thumb and cast on 1 st at hand edge = 24 sts. Work in rounds of vertical stripes for 1-1/4" (3 cm). Shape top: Sl 1, k1, psso with red, 7 sts foll chart, with red, k2 tog, k1, sl 1, k1, psso, 7 sts foll chart, with red k2 tog, k1. Rep these dec once every 2nd round and twice every round. Work dec above previous ones. There should be 2 sts between decs. Work the last dec round with red. Break yarn and thread through rem 8 sts and fasten off. Work left mitt the same, reversing shaping.

FINISHING: Block all pieces. Cut a piece of fabric to the same measurements as the hand towel, pot holder and two pieces for the mitt with

CHART 1

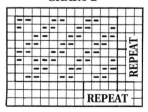

CHART 2

KEY TO CHARTS

- ➖ = Red
- ⬜ = White
- ➕ = Inc 1 st

1/4" (1 cm) seam allowance. Sew the mitt fabric, right sides together and insert in mitt. Sew along lower edge in blanket stitch with red thread. Beg and end row of sts with 3 satin sts. Make a 1/4" (1 cm) hem along edges of fabric and pin to wrong side of pot holder and hand towels and blanket stitch around edges. Make a loop and sew to each piece as shown in photo.

Chart 3

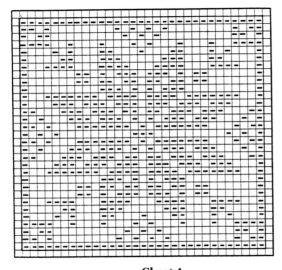

Chart 4

Chart 5

Chart 6

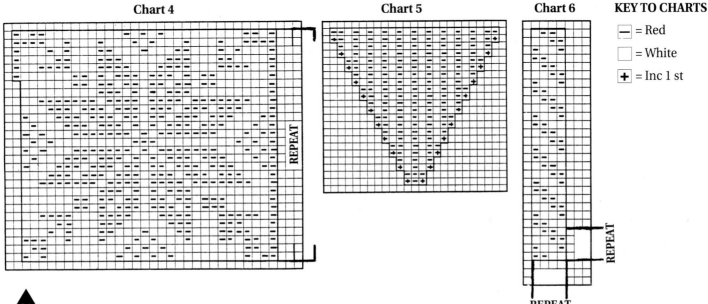

REPEAT

REPEAT

REPEAT

KEY TO CHARTS

─ = Red

☐ = White

✚ = Inc 1 st

Heart Sachet

FINISHED MEASUREMENTS

5-1/2" x 5-1/2" (14 x 14 cm)

*Pattern for Heart Sachet
(photocopy at 200%)*

2nd row, inc 1 st twice. At each edge of every 3rd row, inc 1 st once. At each edge of every 2nd row, inc 1 st 11 times. At each edge of every 3rd row, inc 1 st once. At each edge of every 2nd row, inc 1 st once. At each edge of every 3rd row, inc 1 st twice = 39 sts and 17 ridges = 4-3/4" (12 cm). Dec 1 st at each edge of next row. Bind off the center st. Join a 2nd ball to 2nd half and work at the same time. At each outer edge on every 4th row, dec 1 st once. At each outer

edge on every 2nd row, dec 1 st twice. At each outer edge on every row, dec 1 st twice. At the same time, at each inner edge of every 2nd row, dec 1 st once, on foll row, dec 1 st once, on every 2nd row, dec 1 st once, on every row dec 1 st 3 times. Bind off rem 7 sts on each side. Make a 2nd piece. Place the two pieces together and sew around, leaving an opening at point. Stuff and close opening. With white, crochet 1 row sc around. Fasten off.

▼ Materials

Mayflower Cotton 8 (50 g) 1 ball Pink and White; U.S. size 4 (3.5 mm) knitting needles, U.S. size B/1 (2.5 mm) crochet hook; stuffing

▼ Gauge

U.S. size 4 (3.5 mm) needles in garter st: 4" (10 cm) = 24 sts x 48 rows.

U.S. size 4 (3.5 mm) needles in St st: 4" (10 cm) = 24 sts x 36 rows.

To save time, take time to check gauge!

▼ Directions

BACK: With pink, cast on 3 sts and work garter st. At each edge of every

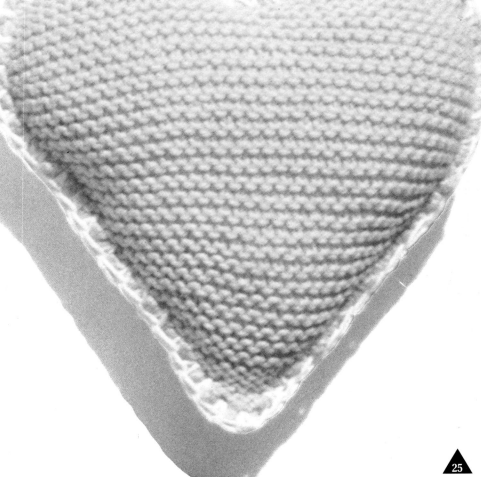

New Baby Welcome

Newborn Gift Set

▼ Materials

Mayflower Cotton 10 (50 g) 4 balls
White; U.S. size 2 (2.5 mm) knitting
needles; 3 buttons, white ribbon

▼ Gauge

U.S. size 2 (2.5 mm) needles in St st: 4"
(10 cm) = 33 sts x 40 rows.

To save time, take time to check gauge!

▼ Stitches Used

EYELET STITCH: Worked over 2 sts
and 3 rows foll chart. When the eyelets
beg on the right side of work, work as
foll: Row 1: P2. Row 2: K2, yo. Row 3:
P2. When the first row of eyelets beg on
the wrong side of work. Row 1: K2. Row
2: Yo, p2 tog. Row 3: K2. Work eyelets
by foll chart.

▼ Directions

PULLOVER

FRONT: Cast on 88 (92, 96) sts and
work 3/4" (2 cm) in 1/1 ribbing, end
wrong side of work row.

Work 4 rows in St st, then work 6 rows
in eyelet st by foll chart 1, beg and end
row with 1 border st. Right side: Row 1:
1 border st, *p2, k2*, rep * to *, end with
p2, 1 border st. Row 2: 1 border st, *k2
tog, yo, p2*, rep * to *, end with k2 tog,
1 border st. Row 3: Like row 1. Row 4:
(Wrong side of work): Like row 1. Row
5: 1 border st, *k2, yo, p2 tog*, rep * to *
end with k2, 1 border st. Row 6: Like
row 1. Continue in St st until piece
measures 4-1/2" (4-3/4", 5") - 11.5 (12,
12.5) cm. Shape Raglans: Bind off 2 sts
at beg of next 2 rows = 84 (88, 92) sts.
Dec 1 st at each edge of every 2nd row

19 (20, 21) times as foll: 1 border st, sl 1,
k1, psso, work to last 3 sts, k2 tog, 1
border st. (Note: For last dec, bind off
border st with last dec.) With the first
raglan dec, work in eyelet st centering
chart 2. Work edge sts in St st. The
chart is 21 rows high = 7 eyelets. Place
rem 44 (46, 48) sts on a holder.

LEFT BACK: Cast on 42 (44, 46) sts and
work 3/4" (2 cm) as foll: 1 border st, 36
(38, 40) sts in 1/1 ribbing, 5 sts in garter
st, end with wrong side row. Continue
in St st, maintaining 5 sts in garter st as
established. Work 4 rows over the 36
(38, 40) sts in St st, then work 6 rows of
eyelet border foll chart 1, beg at point
1(2,1). Continue in St st until piece
measures 4-1/2" (4-3/4", 5") - 11 (12,
12.5) cm. At left edge, bind off 2 sts. At
left edge of every 2nd row, dec 1 st as
on front. Bind off border st with last
dec. Place rem 20 (21, 22) sts on holder.

RIGHT BACK: Work same as left back,
but when raglan measures 2" (2-1/4",
2-1/2") - 5 (5.5, 6) cm and 3-1/4" (3-
1/4", 3-1/2") - 8 (8.5, 9) cm, make a
buttonhole in the garter st section. For
each buttonhole, bind off 2 sts. On foll
row, cast on 2 sts over bound off sts.

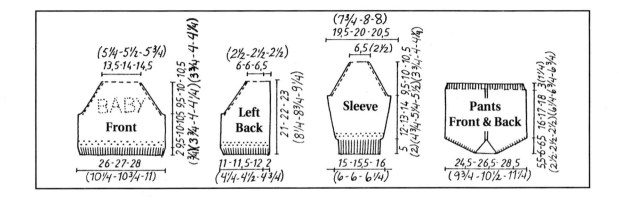

SLEEVE: Cast on 42 (44, 46) sts, work 2" (5 cm) in 1/1 ribbing. Continue in St st, inc 10 sts evenly spaced across first row = 52 (54, 56) sts. After 6 rows, work eyelet st foll chart 1, beg with point 2 (1, 2). At the same time, inc 1 st each edge of every 6th row 7 times. Work new sts in St st as you inc = 66 (68, 70) sts.

When sleeve measures 6-3/4" (7-1/4", 7-1/2") - 17 (18, 19) cm from beg, shape raglan. Bind off 2 sts at beg of next 2 rows. Dec 1 st at each edge of every 2nd row as on back. Bind off border sts with last dec. Place rem 22 sts on holder.

FINISHING: Sew raglan seams. Neckband: Pick up sts from left back, sleeve, front, sleeve and right back and work as foll: 5 sts in garter st, 118 (122, 126) sts in 1/1 ribbing, 5 sts in garter st. After the 2nd row, work in eyelet st as foll: 5 rows in garter st, *k1, yo, k2 tog*, rep * to *, end with k1 (2, 0), 5 sts in garter st, making the last buttonhole over the center 2 sts of garter st. When border measures 1/2" (1.5 cm). Bind off. Sew sleeve seams, rev seam for sleeve cuff. Make a cord and thread through eyelets at neckband. Reinforce buttonholes and sew on buttons. Fold cuffs to outside.

PANTS

FRONT: Cast on 88 (94, 100) sts and work 1 row on wrong side as foll: 1 border st, 31 (33, 35) sts in 1/1 ribbing, beg with p1, p 24 (26, 28) sts (St st) for crotch, 31 (33, 35) sts in 1/1 ribbing, beg with p1, end with 1 border st. On the 2nd and 4th row, dec 1 st at each edge of crotch: Knit the last rib st with the first st of crotch and the last st of crotch with the first st of ribbing as you work across. After 5 rows, continue in St st across all sts. On the 2nd row, dec 1 st at each edge of crotch. At the same

time, at each edge of every 2nd row, inc 1 st by knitting in the strand between the border st and the first and last sts of row. After the last crotch dec, you will have 84 (90, 96) sts (1 st at center between decs). Continue the side incs on every 2nd row and dec 1 st at each edge of center 2 sts. When piece measures 6-1/4" (6-3/4", 7") - 16 (17, 18) cm measured at the side seam, work in short rows, continuing center dec and omitting edge decs. Beg 2 sts from the side seam, work to last 2 sts, turn and work to last 4 sts, turn and work to last 4 sts and continue in this way until 6 sts rem at the center. Work 1 row across all 62 (66, 70) sts, then work 1/2" (1.5 cm) in eyelet st: 1 border st, *k2 tog, yo, k2 tog*, rep * to * across, end with 1 border st. Work the foll row by purling all the yo's. Continue in 1/1 ribbing. When ribbing measures 1-1/4" (3 cm), bind off all sts.

BACK: Work same as front.

FINISHING: Sew side seams and crotch seam. Make a cord. Thread cord though waistband eyelets.

BOOTIES

Beg at top edge and work border pat foll chart 3 as foll: Row 1: 1 border st, *k2, yo, k2 tog, p1, yo, k6, k3 tog, k6, yo, p1*, rep * to * twice, end with k2, yo, k2 tog, 1 border st. Row 2: 1 border st, p2, yo, p2 tog, *k1, p1, yo, p5, p3 tog, p5, yo, p1, k1, p2, yo, p2 tog*, rep * to * twice, end with 1 border st. Work rows 3 to 6 by foll chart.

Cast on 69 sts. Row 1: 1 border st, knit to last st, 1 border st. Row 2: (right side): 1 border st, *k2, yo*, rep * to *, end with k1, 1 border st. Row 3: Like row 1, but knit each yo of previous row.

Work in border pattern, working the 6 rows twice. Knit 1 row, dec 13 sts evenly spaced across row = 56 sts. Continue in 1/1 ribbing, working eyelets on 5th row as foll: 1 border st, *yo, k2 tog, p1, k1*, rep * to *, end with 1 yo, k2 tog, 1 border st. Work 2nd row of pat by purling the yo's. Place 21 sts on each edge on holders and work the center 14 sts for 4 rows: 1 border st, 10 sts in St st, 1 border st. Work 6 rows of eyelet pat twice, foll chart 1, beg at point 1 and end with 4 rows in St st. Break yarn. Pick up 21 sts from side, 10 sts from side of top of foot, 14 sts from top of foot, 10 sts from side of top, pick up 21 sts from side = 76 sts. Work 2 rows of St st, 2 rows of rev St st, 2 rows of St st, 3 rows of eyelet st foll chart 1, beg at point 1, 2 rows of St st, 2 rows of rev St st. Continue in St st for the sole: Row 1: Right side of work: 1 border st, k5, k3 tog, k21, sl 1, k2 tog, psso, k10, k3 tog, k21, sl 1, k2 tog, psso, k5, 1 border st = 68 sts. Row 2: Purl. Row 3: 1 border st, k3, k3 tog, k21, sl 1, k2 tog, psso, k6, k3 tog, k21, sl 1, k2 tog, psso, k3, 1 border st = 60 sts. Row 4: Purl. Row 5: 1 border st, k1, k3 tog, k21, sl 1, k2 tog, psso, k2, k3 tog, k21, sl 1, k2 tog, psso, k1, 1 border st = 52 sts. Row 6: Purl. Row 7: 1 border st, k2 tog, k21, sl 1, k1, k2 tog, k21, sl 1, k1, psso, 1 border st = 48 sts. Row 8: Purl. Bind off all sts. Make a 2nd bootie in the same way, but beg chart at point 2. Sew back and sole seam. Thead ribbon through eyelets.

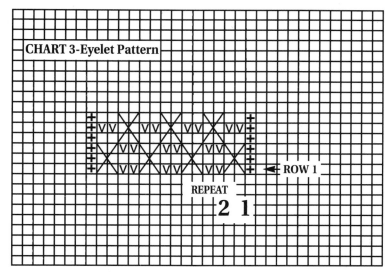

CHART 3-Eyelet Pattern

← ROW 1

REPEAT

2 1

KEY TO CHARTS

+	= 1 border st
⋈	= 1 eyelet over 2 sts and 3 rows high
v	= k1
—	= p1
◣	= k2 tog
╲	= p2 tog
○	= yo
▲	= k3 tog
△	= p3 tog

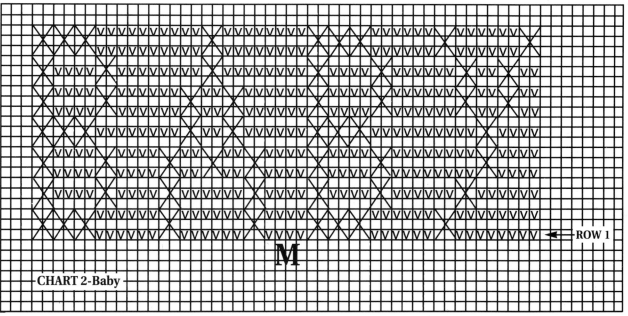

← ROW 1

M

CHART 2-Baby

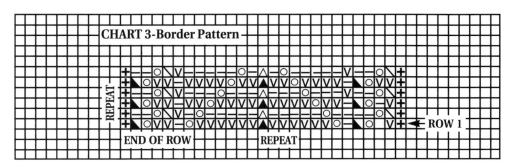

CHART 3-Border Pattern

REPEAT

← ROW 1

END OF ROW   REPEAT

29

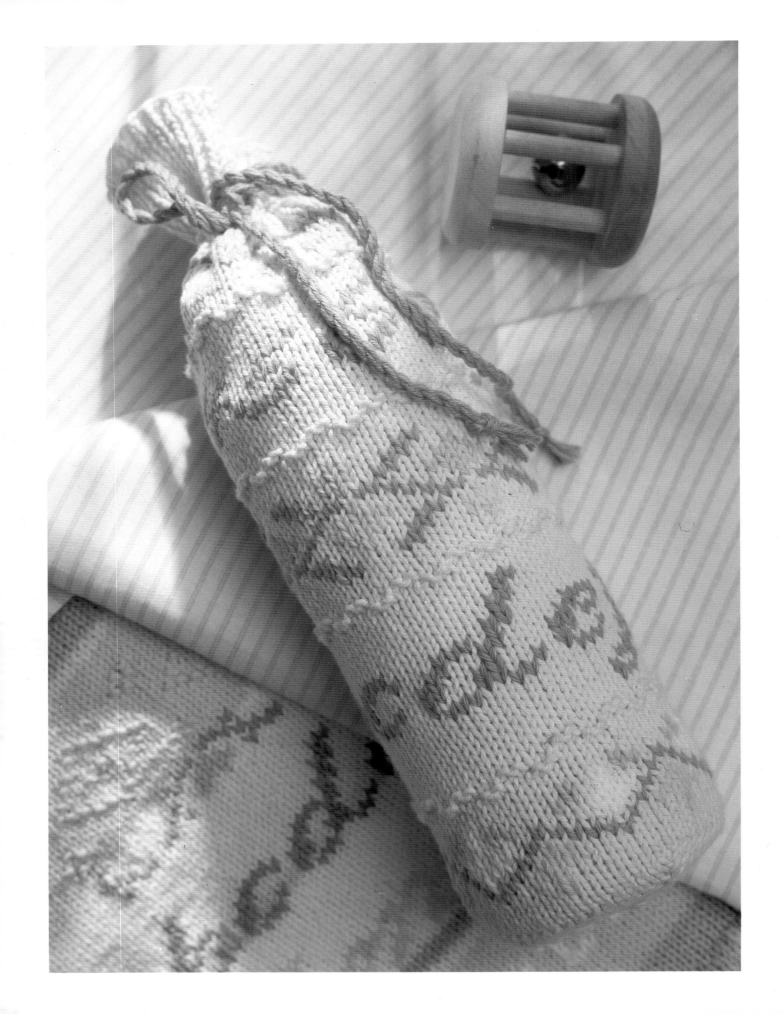

Baby Bottle Warmer

FINISHED MEASUREMENTS

Height 12-1/4" (31 cm)

▼ Materials

Mayflower Cotton 8 (50 g) 2 balls Yellow and small amounts of Light Blue, Blue, Green, White and Pink; U.S. size 2 and 3 (2.5 and 3 mm) knitting needles

▼ Gauge

U.S. size 3 (3 mm) needles in St st: 4" (10 cm) = 26 sts x 32 rows.

To save time, take time to check gauge!

▼ Directions

BACK: With larger size needles and yellow, cast on 60 sts and work in St st by foll chart, beg and end with 1 border st. After the last row of chart, work one eyelet row as foll: 1 border st, *k2 tog, yo*, rep * to *, end with 1 border st. Change to smaller size needles and work 1-1/4" (3 cm) of 1/1 ribbing. Work 2 rows of pink and 1 row of yellow. Bind off loosely with yellow. With larger size needles and yellow, pick up 58 sts from lower edge of piece. Work as foll: Row 1: 1 border st, k6, k2 tog, k12, k2 tog, k12, k2 tog, k12, k2 tog, k6, 1 border st. Rows 2 to 13: Dec 4 sts on every row, working dec above previous dec. On the last row, bind off the border st with last dec. Thread yarn through rem 8 sts, leaving a long end to sew side seam. Embroider the piece by foll chart. Work each pattern motif as foll: pat motif 1 repeat has 10 sts. Pat motif 2 repeat has 17 sts. Pat motif 3 repeat has 10 sts. Sew the bottom and side seams. Make a blue cord 30" (75 cm) long and thread through eyelets.

KEY TO CHART

- L = Pink
- ⁄ = Light Blue
- X = Blue
- + = Green
- · = White
- ☐ = With yellow, knit on the right side, purl on the wrong side
- V = With yellow, purl on the right side, knit on the wrong side

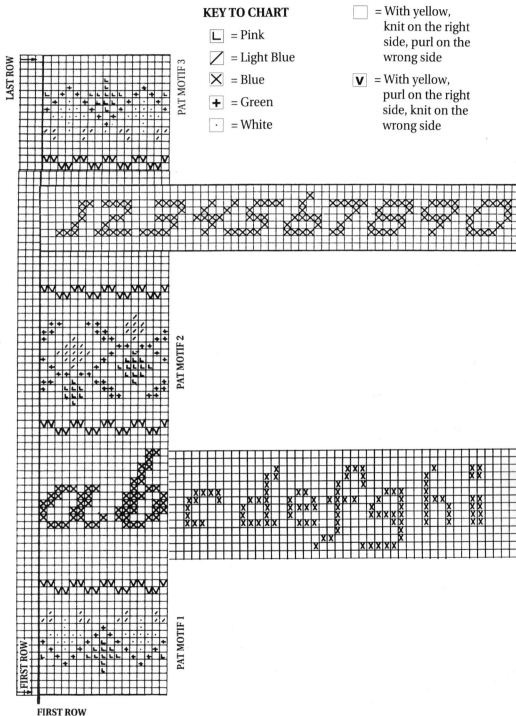

LAST ROW

PAT MOTIF 3

PAT MOTIF 2

FIRST ROW

FIRST ROW

PAT MOTIF 1

Pig & Chicken Bibs

▼ Materials

Mayflower Cotton 8 (50 g) for Pig Bib:
1 ball each White, Blue, Light Pink,
Yellow and Pink; for Chick Bib: 1 ball
each White, Yellow, Blue, Pink, and
Dark Yellow; U.S. size 3 (3 mm) knitting
needles

▼ Gauge

U.S. size 3 (3 mm) needles in St st: 4" =
26 sts x 36 rows.

To save time, take time to check gauge!

▼ Directions

With white, cast on 32 sts and work in
St st. At beg of 3rd, 4th, 5th and 6th row,
cast on 3 sts = 44 sts. Work 77 rows from
beg, then bind off center 14 sts. Join 2nd
ball of yarn to 2nd part and work at the
same time. At each neck edge of every
row, bind off 3 sts once, bind off 2 sts
once, dec 1 st twice. At the same time,
at side edge of every 2nd row, dec 1 st 3
times. Bind off rem 5 sts. With blue or
pink, cast on 8 sts and work in garter st.
Make one piece 7" (18 cm) long for neck
border and one piece 44" (110 cm) long
for sides. Bind off.

FINISHING: Embroider motifs at center
foll chart, beg the pig motif on the 10th
row and the chick on the 13th row. Fold
the borders in half and sew short piece to
neck edge and long piece around sides,
extending for ties. Sew ends.

KEY TO CHARTS

1 = White	— = Yellow		
● = Blue	= = Pink		
╱ = Light Pink	╲ = Dark Yellow		

CHART for Chicken

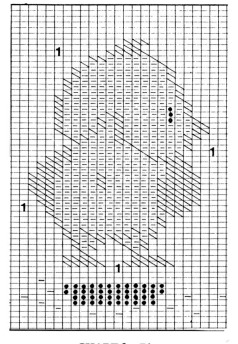

CHART for Pig

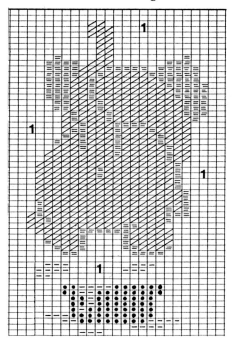

Announcement Pullovers

FINISHED MEASUREMENTS

Sizes 3 (6, 12) months

Chest 20-3/4" (22", 23") - 52 (55, 58) cm

Length 10" (10-1/2", 11") - 25 (26.5, 28) cm

Sleeve Length 6-3/4" (7-1/4", 8") - 17 (18.5, 20) cm

▼ Materials

Mayflower Cotton 8 (50 g) 2 balls Pink or Green - MC, 2 balls White, 1 ball Gray; U.S. size 2 and 3 (2 and 3 mm) knitting needles, 2 decorative snaps

▼ Gauge

U.S. size 3 (3 mm) needles in fairisle St st: 4" (10 cm) = 26 sts x 31 rows.

U.S. size 3 (3 mm) needles in St st: 4" (10 cm) = 26 sts x 36 rows.

To save time, take time to check gauge!

▼ Directions

BACK: With smaller size needles and MC, cast on 70 (74, 78) sts and work 3/4" (2 cm) in St st, then work 1 eyelet row as foll: 1 border st, *k2 tog, yo*, rep * to * across, end with 1 border st. Purl the foll row, purling all yo's. Work 1/4" (1 cm) of St st, end on right side of work row. With a spare needle, pick up each st of cast on row and purl 1 st from cast on row and 1 st from needle together across. Change to larger size needles, work in St st until piece measures 10" (10-1/2", 11") - 25 (26.5, 28) cm from beg, end with right side row. Work 1 eyelet row as before and 3/4" (2 cm) of St st. Bind off all sts.

(continued on page 38)

CHART for Baby Boy Pullover Front

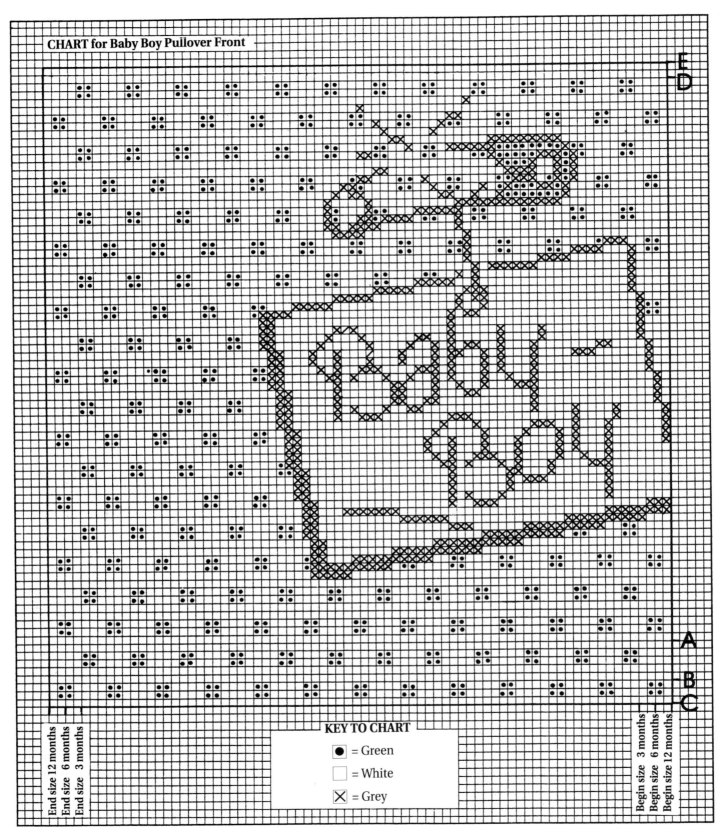

E
D

A
B
C

End size 12 months
End size 6 months
End size 3 months

KEY TO CHART

● = Green

☐ = White

✖ = Grey

Begin size 3 months
Begin size 6 months
Begin size 12 months

CHART for Baby Girl Pullover Front

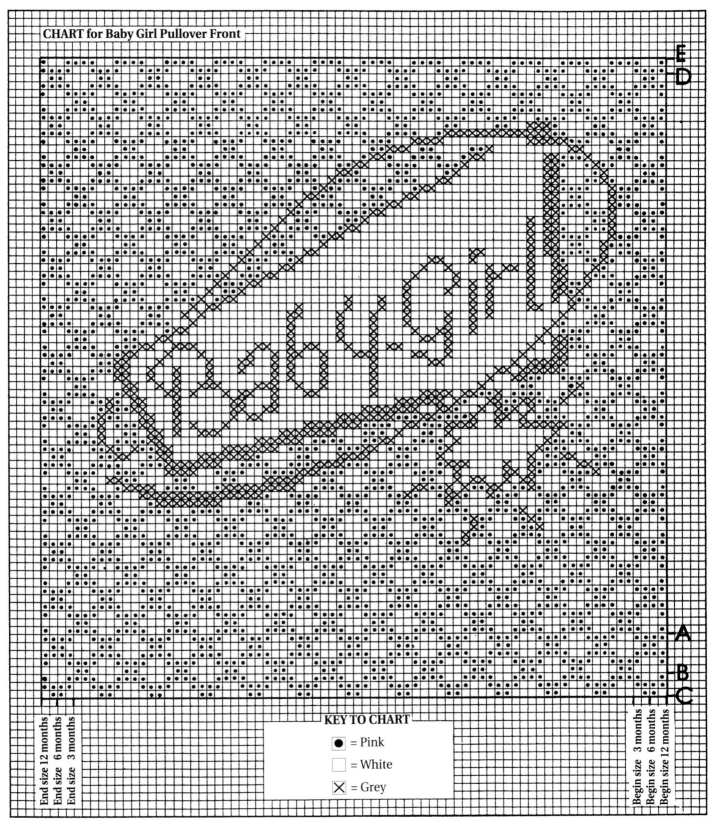

SLEEVE CHART for Girl

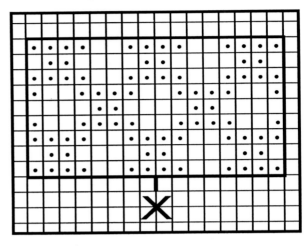

KEY TO CHART

● = Pink or Blue
☐ = White
☒ = Center

(continued from page 35)

FRONT: Beg front same as back in white. Change to larger size needles and work by foll chart for baby boy or girl. Carry unused yarn loosely across wrong side of work row. Embroider the gray letters and border in duplicate stitch on finished work. Beg the first row with A (B, C) and work through D (D, E). When the piece measures 10" (10-1/2", 11") - 25 (26.5, 28) cm from beg, work 3/4" (2 cm) of St st, 1 eyelet row and 3/4" (2 cm) of St st. Bind off loosely.

SLEEVE: With smaller size needles and white, cast on 34 (36, 38) sts, work 1/4" in St st, 1 eyelet row, 1/4" of St st and purl 1 row as on back.

Change to larger size needles, work in jacquard St st by centering chart at point X. Inc 1 st each edge of every 3rd row 12 (10, 10) times. Inc 1 st each edge of every 4th row 1 (4, 5) times. Work new sts in pat st as you inc = 60 (64, 68) sts.

When sleeve measures 6-3/4" (7-1/4", 7-3/4") - 17 (18.5, 20) cm from beg, bind off all sts.

NECKBAND: Embroider the letters and border in gray. Turn at eyelet row and hem. Place the back hem over the front and baste in place. Sew the sleeves to side seams, matching the center of the sleeve with the center of the shoulder. Sew side and sleeve seams. 1-3/4" (2", 2-1/4") - 4.5 (5, 5.5) cm from the side seam, attach a decorative snap to each shoulder. See photo.

SLEEVE CHART for Boy

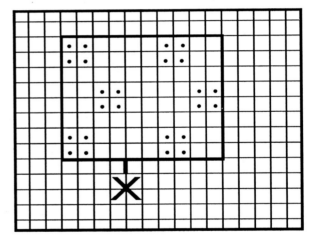

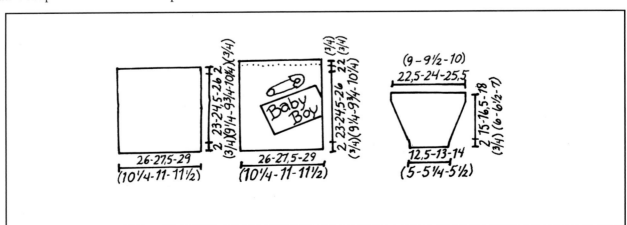

Rooster Bib

▼ Materials

Mayflower Cotton 8 (50 g) 1 ball Orange, small amounts of White, Red and Brown DMC embroidery floss; U.S. size 3 (3 mm) knitting needles, U.S. size C/2 (2 mm) crochet hook

▼ Gauge

U.S. size 3 (3 mm) needles in St st: 4" (10 cm) = 26 sts x 36 rows

To save time, take time to check gauge!

▼ Directions

With orange, cast on 48 sts and work 6 rows in garter st (= 3 ridges). Continue as foll: 3 sts in garter st, 42 sts in St st, 3 sts in garter st. Work until piece measures 8-1/4" (21 cm). Now work as foll: 3 sts in garter st, 7 sts of St st, 28 sts of garter st, 7 sts in St st, 3 sts in garter st. After 8 rows, bind off the center 22 sts. Join a 2nd ball to 2nd half and work at the same time. When piece measures 11" (28 cm) from beg, work 6 rows of garter st. Bind off all sts. At neck edge corners of top of bib, attach yarn and with crochet hook, make an 8" (20 cm) long chain. Fasten off. Embroider 2 chickens foll chart, placing them as you desire. See photo.

KEY TO CHART

- ■ = Brown   DMC 838
- ✕ = Red   DMC 321
- ☐ = Yellow DMC 742
- — = White

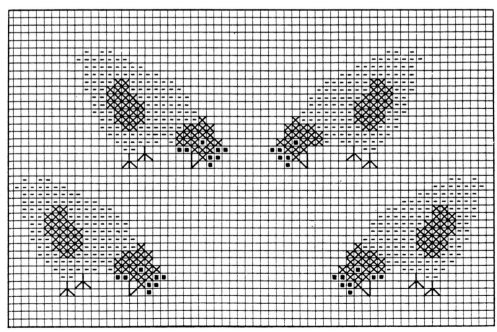

Adults

Ties

FINISHED MEASUREMENTS

Bow Tie Length
4-1/2" (11.5 cm)

Bow Tie Width
1-1/2" (4 cm)

Tie Length
52-3/4" (132 cm)

Tie Width
1-1/2" (4 cm)

▼ Materials

BOW TIE

Tapestry Wool: For Yellow/Red/Black tie: 10 g Yellow, 5 g Black and 5 g Red. For the Green/White/Black tie: 5 g Black, 5 g Green and 5 g White

TIE

Tapestry Wool: For the Red/Green tie, 30 g Red and 15 g Green; for the Black/White tie, 25 g Black and 15 g White; for the Green/Blue/Red tie, 5 g Red, 15 g Blue, 20 g Green; for the Red/Green/Black/White tie, 20 g Red, 15 g Green, 5 g Black and 5 g White

U.S. size 1 (2 mm) knitting needles

▼ Gauge

U.S. size 1 (2 mm) needles in St st: 4" (10 cm) = 46 sts x 46 rows.

To save time, take time to check gauge!

▼ Directions

BOW TIE

Cast on 3 sts in MC. Work in fairisle St st by foll chart, beg and end with 1 border st. Carry unused yarn loosely across wrong side of work. Inc 1 st at each edge of every row 27 times. Work the incs by working 2 sts in the border sts. Work the inc sts in fairisle. After 27 rows, you will have 57 sts on the needle. Continue inc at right edge, but dec on left edge. Dec by working the 2 sts at left edge tog. Work until piece measures 9-1/4" (23 cm), measured at the right edge. Continue by dec at both edges on every row 27 times = 3 sts. Bind off. Cast on 3 sts in MC and work in fairisle by foll chart, beg and end with 1 border st. Inc at each edge of every row 11 times, working new sts in fairisle St st = 25 sts. Continue by inc at right edge, but dec 1 st at left edge. When piece measures 2-1/2" (6 cm), measured at right edge, continue dec at both edges 11 times = 3 sts. Bind off.

FINISHING: Embroider the lines in duplicate st. Block lightly. Sew the short ends of tie together to form circle. Fold in half lengthwise wrong sides tog so that the seam is on the center back.

Turn right side out. Sew seam. Sew small piece in the same manner. Fold the small piece over the center of the large piece and sew in place.

TIE

With MC, cast on 30 sts and work in fairisle St st by foll chart, beg and end with 1 border st. At right edge of every row, inc 1 st 28 times as on bow tie. Work inc sts in pat. After 28 rows, you will have 58 sts. Continue incs at right edge and beg dec 1 st at left edge of every row until piece measures 52-3/4" (132 cm), measured at right edge, continue dec at left edge and work right edge even. After 28 rows, you will have 30 sts on needle. Bind off loosely.

FINISHING: Embroider the lines in duplicate st. Block lightly. Fold in half lengthwise wrong sides tog so that the seam is at the center back. Sew seam. Fold the pointed end inside tie and sew in place.

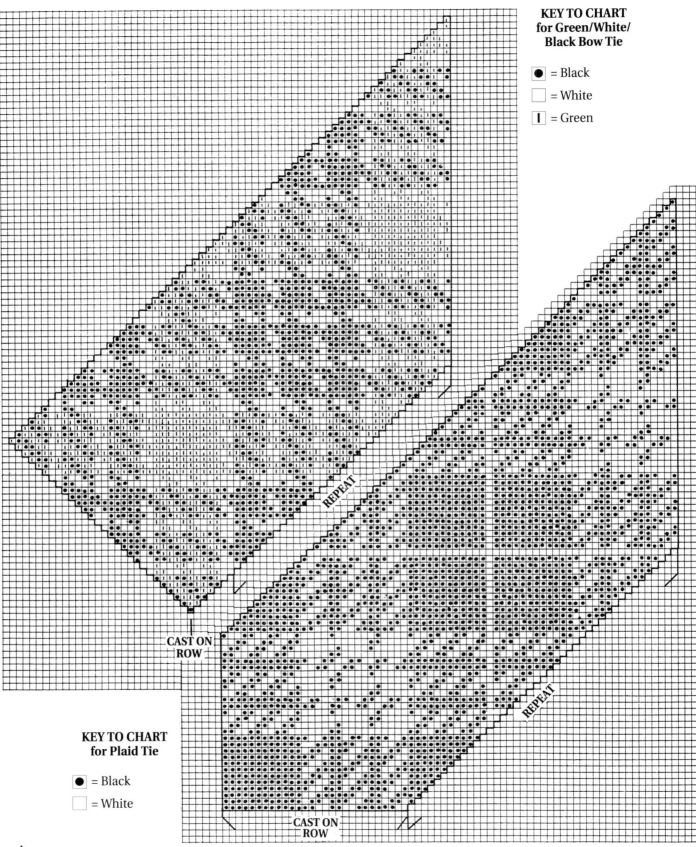

**KEY TO CHART
for Green/White/
Black Bow Tie**

● = Black

☐ = White

❘ = Green

REPEAT

REPEAT

**CAST ON
ROW**

**KEY TO CHART
for Plaid Tie**

● = Black

☐ = White

**CAST ON
ROW**

Bracelets

▼ Materials

Raffia in desired colors, U.S. size 10 (6 mm) knitting needles

▼ Gauge

U.S. size 10 (6 mm) needles in St st: 4" (10 cm) = 13 sts x 18 rows.

To save time, take time to check gauge!

▼ Directions

Cast on 30 sts and work in St st for 3-1/4" (8 cm) for the small bracelet or 5-1/2" (14 cm) for large. Bind off. Fold in half lengthwise with right sides together. Turn wrong side out and sew ends to form ring.

Floral Gloves

▼ Materials

Neveda Primula Fine (50 g) 1 ball White, U.S. size 2 (2.5 mm) double-pointed knitting needles, embroidery floss in Red, Dark Red, Yellow, Light Yellow, Blue and Green

▼ Gauge

U.S. size 2 (2.5 mm) needles in St st: 4" (10 cm) = 26 sts x 36 rows.

To save time, take time to check gauge!

▼ Directions

LEFT HAND: With white, cast on 50 sts and work in rounds for 2-3/4" (7 cm) in 1/1 ribbing. Continue in St st, inc 6 sts evenly spaced around = 56 sts. After 4 rounds, shape thumb: Mark beg of round. Work 54 sts, inc 1 st in the strand between sts and work last 2 sts of round. Foll round: Work without inc. Inc on foll round. Inc at each edge of inc sts as foll: Work to 1 st before first inc st, inc 1, work to last inc st, inc 1. Rep these incs every 2nd round so that there are 2 more sts between each inc = 17 incs for thumb. Place on a holder. Continue in rounds, casting on 6 sts in place of the thumb sts. Dec 6 sts over the next 6 rounds as foll: On every 2nd round, knit the first and last sts tog of

each round = 56 sts. Work for 2" (5 cm) from thumb, then work for fingers. Work the first 9 sts of the round, cast on 2 sts, pick up last 8 sts of round = 19 sts and place other sts on holder. Work these 19 sts for index finger for 2-1/2" (6 cm) to desired finger length. Dec 5 sts evenly spaced around. K2 tog around. Break yarn and thread through rem 7 sts. Fasten off. For middle finger, pick up 7 sts from top of hand, cast on 2 sts, pick up 6 sts from palm, inc 1 st, cast on 2 sts from index finger, inc 1 st = 19 sts . Work in rounds for 2-3/4" (7 cm), then shape top as before. For ring finger, pick up 7 sts from top of hand, pick up 2 sts, work 6 sts from palm, inc 1, cast on 2 sts from middle finger, inc 1 = 19 sts and work as middle finger. For little finger, pick up 7 sts from top, pick up last 6 sts from palm, inc 1 st, pick up 2 sts from ring finger, inc 1 st = 17 sts and work in rounds for 2" (5 cm) and dec 5 sts around. On the foll round, k2 tog. Break yarn and thread through rem 6 sts. Fasten off. Pick up 17 sts for thumb, pick up 6 sts from hand = 23 sts. On foll round, dec 3 over the 6 = 20 sts. Work 2-1/2" (6 cm). Dec 4 sts on foll round = 16 sts. K2 tog around = 8 sts. Break yarn and thread through rem sts. Fasten off.

RIGHT HAND: Work same as left hand, working thumb at beg of round. (Work 2 sts, inc 1 and so on.)

FINISHING: Trace motif on tracing paper. Pin to the top of hand, placing the motif above the ribbing. Embroider motif as foll: Embroider lines in stem st and the leaves in satin st. Embroider in colors as shown in photo. Trim excess tracing paper. Embroider the top of the fingers and thumb in V motifs in red, dark red, yellow and blue.

GLOVE MOTIF

SHOWN 80% OF ACTUAL SIZE

Colorful Mittens and Scarf

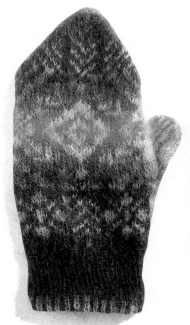
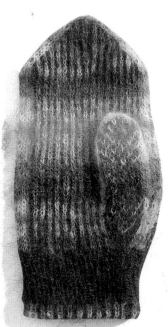

▼ Materials

Kid Mohair (50 g) 1 ball each Dark Brown, Brown, White, Purple, Light Yellow, Yellow, Green, Turquoise, Gray Blue, Dark Red, Red, Pink and Salmon; U.S. size 2 and 3 (2.5 and 3 mm) double pointed knitting needles

▼ Gauge

U.S. size 3 (3 mm) needles in St st: 4" (10 cm) = 28 sts x 30 rows.

To save time, take time to check gauge!

▼ Directions

RIGHT MITTEN

With smaller size needles and dark brown, cast on 64 sts and knit 1 round, dec 12 sts evenly spaced across first round = 52 sts. Work 10 rounds foll chart 4. With larger size needles, work 1 round in dark brown in 1/1 ribbing. Change to smaller size needles and work for 1-1/2" (4 cm), turn and knit 1 round, inc 12 sts = 64 sts. Mark beg of round. Change to larger size needles and work from point A to B foll chart 5, 3 sts from point B to C foll chart 6 = thumb and 60 sts from point C to D foll chart 5. Beg the foll round with the inc for the thumb. Work the first inc as foll: Work 1 st of chart 5, then work chart 6,

inc 1 st in the strand between sts, work 3 sts in pat st, inc 1 st, foll chart 5 from point C to D. Work these inc at each edge of thumb on every 2nd round 3 times and on every 3rd round twice. After the last inc, you will have 76 sts on needles. Work these sts to point X on both charts. Foll round: Work the first st of the round, place 15 sts on a holder for thumb and cast on 13 sts, work to end of round = 74 sts. Work by foll chart 5, work now from point A to D and in height from X to Y. Work the first dec round for top as foll: k1, sl 1, k1, psso, 32 sts of established pattern, k2 tog, k1, sl 1, k1, psso, 32 sts of established pattern in chart, k2 tog. Work these dec on every round. Work the dec above the previous decreases with 1 st between the decreases. Make the dec in the same color as the knit sts. Break the yarn and thread through rem sts. Thumb: Pick up

15 sts from the thumb and cast on 13 sts at hand edge = 28 sts and work in rounds foll chart 6 from point X. Shape the top as on mitten. Bind off. Left Mitten: Work same as right mitten, rev placement of thumb and patterns. Fold the brown 1/1 ribbing border to inside and slip st in place.

SCARF

Work in rounds of fairisle St st by foll charts. Background color for chart 1 is dark brown, chart 2 is as foll: 60 rounds in dark brown, 10 rounds in brown, 10 rounds in dark brown, 10 rounds in brown, 12 rounds in dark brown, 50 rounds in brown, 6 rounds in purple, 16 rounds in brown, 32 rounds in purple, 6 rounds in dark red, 10 rounds in purple, 60 rounds in dark red, 6 rounds in red, 10 rounds in dark red, 32 rounds in red and chart 3 in red.

Colorful Mittens and Scarf

Cast on 120 sts and dark brown, purl 1
round, knit 1 round, purl 1 round, then
continue in St st. Mark beg of round.
Work 4 rounds foll chart 1, 1 round in
dark brown, then foll chart 2. Work the
chart 2, 4 times across and 11 times in
height, knit 1 round in red, work 4
rounds foll chart 3 and continue in red:
knit 1 round, purl 1 round, purl 1 round.
Bind off in red. Sew ends.

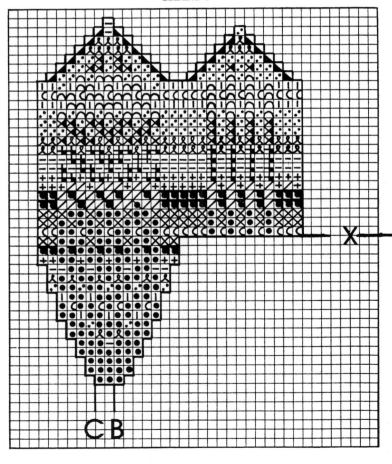

CHART 1

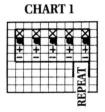

CHART 3

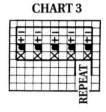

CHART 2

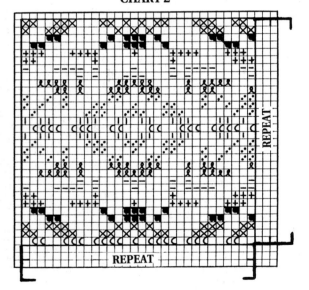

CHART 6

CHART 4

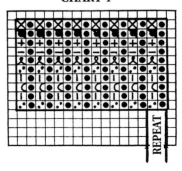

KEY TO CHART
MITTENS

- ◸ = K2 tog
- ◣ = Sl 1, k1, psso
- ╱ = Brown

- ⊠ = Dark red
- ✚ = Purple
- ◠ = Red
- Ⅱ Light yellow
- — = Yellow
- ✚ = Green

- ∴ = White
- ◥ = Turquoise
- Ⅰ = Salmon
- (= Pink
- ✕ = Gray Blue
- ● = Dark brown

KEY TO CHART
SCARF

- Ⅱ Light Yellow
- — = Yellow
- ✚ = Green

- ◥ = Turquoise
- Ⅰ = Salmon
- (= Pink
- ✕ = Gray Blue
- ☐ = Background color
- ∴ = White

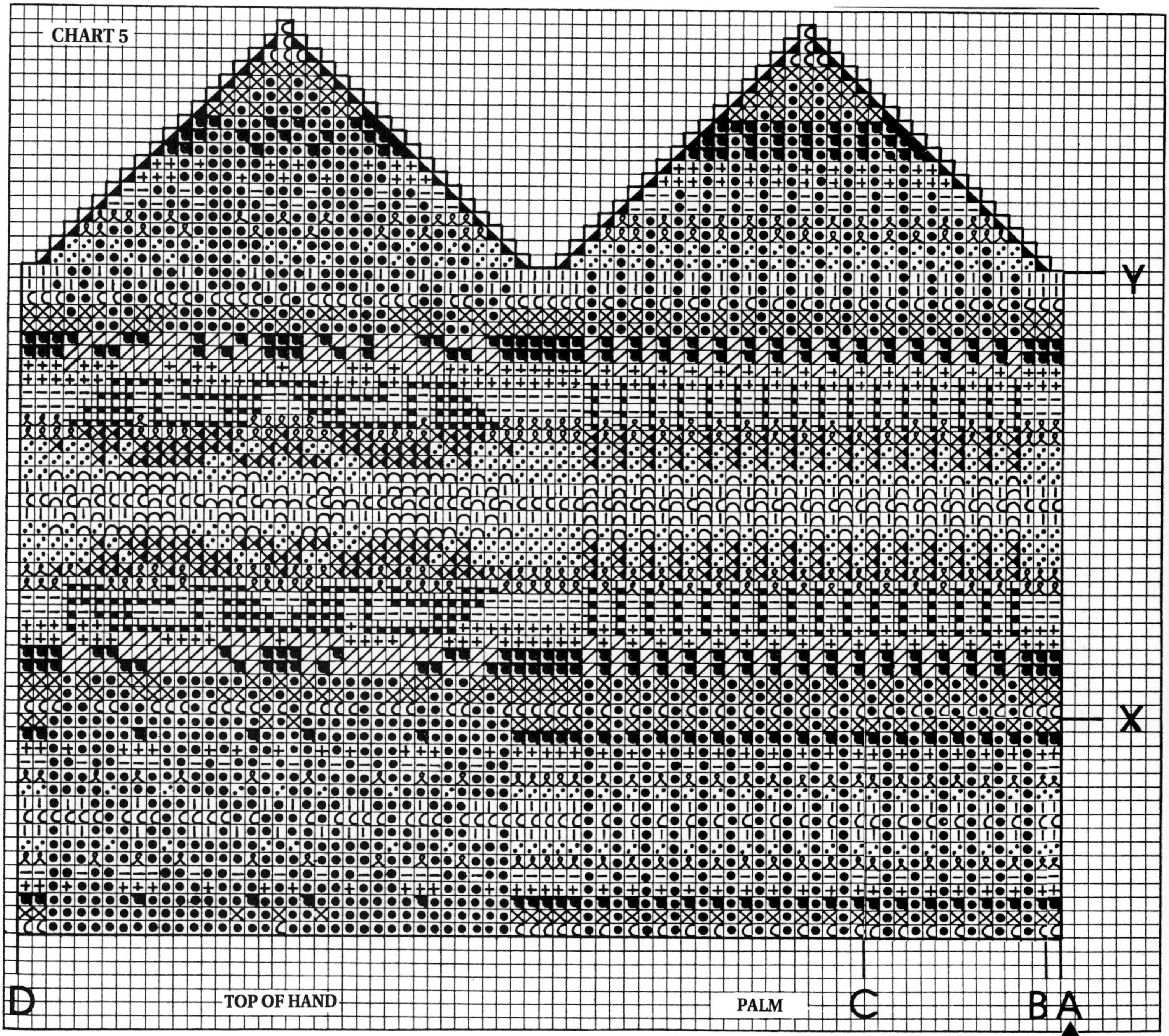

CHART 5

TOP OF HAND   PALM

D   C   B A

51

Classic Pullover

FINISHED MEASUREMENTS

Size
Medium (Large)
Chest
49-1/4" (123 cm)
Length
28-3/4" (72 cm)
Sleeve Length
20" (50 cm)

▼ Materials

Gjestal Polar (100 g) 7 balls Black and 4 balls Ecru, U.S. size 8 and 10 (5 and 6 mm) circular knitting needles, wide bias seam binding

▼ Gauge

U.S. size 10 (6 mm) needles in St st: 4" (10 cm) = 13 sts x 15 rows.

To save time, take time to check gauge!

▼ Directions

BODY: Worked in rounds. Armholes are cut later.

With smaller size needles and black, cast on 142 sts and work 2-1/2" (6 cm) in rounds of 1/1 ribbing, taking care not to twist. Inc 18 sts evenly spaced on last round = 160 sts.

Change to larger size needles, work in jacquard St st by foll chart. Mark the first st of the round. Work from point X to Y, 8 times. Carry unused yarn loosely across back of work. When piece measures 16-3/4" (42 cm) - point A on chart. Inc for armholes as foll: work 80 sts, inc 1 st, work 80 sts, inc 1 st. On next round, inc 1 st at center of back and front so motif will be symmetrical on back and front. At each edge of previous armhole inc, inc 1 st on next 2 rounds = 5 inc sts at each armhole. Work these incs in black. Do not work these sts in jacquard = 172 sts. Work to last round of chart. Piece will measure 28-3/4" (72 cm) from beg. Bind off all sts.

KEY TO CHART - Sleeve

☐ = Black
⬤ = Ecru

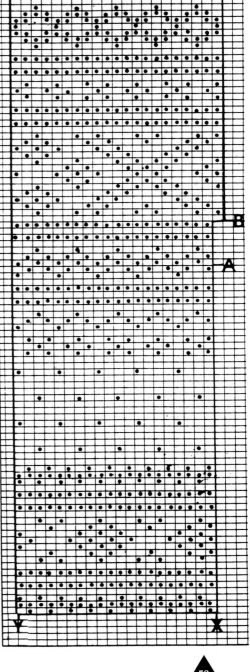

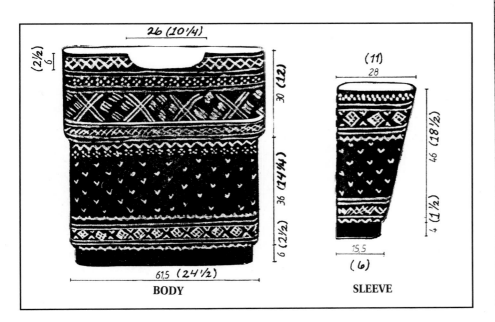

BODY   **SLEEVE**

53

SLEEVE: With smaller size needles and black, cast on 34 sts, work 1-1/2" (4 cm) in rounds of 1/1 ribbing, inc 7 sts evenly spaced on last round = 41 sts.

Change to larger size needles, work in jacquard St st, centering chart at point M. Mark the first and last sts of round. Inc 1 st each edge of these sts every 4th round 16 times. Work new sts in jacquard St st as you inc = 73 sts.

When sleeve measures 20" (50 cm) from beg, bind off loosely.

FINISHING: With sewing machine, sew 2 rows of short sts in a U shape along the armhole edges, leaving 3 sts inside the U. Cut down the center sts. Shape the neck by sewing with short sts. Foll shape of neckline shown on chart, 2-1/2" (6 cm) deep, 10-1/4" (26 cm) wide. Sew shoulder seams. With circular needle and black, pick up and knit 72 sts around neck. Work 1-1/4" (3 cm) in 1/1 ribbing, bind off. Sew sleeves to armholes, leaving cut edges in seam. Sew seam binding around the cut edges.

CHART for Body

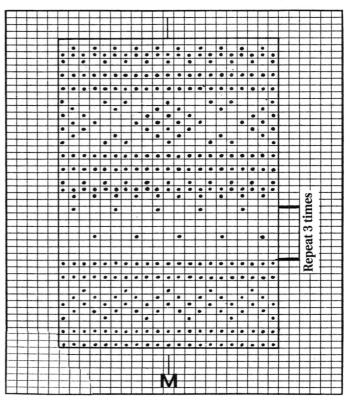

Repeat 3 times

M

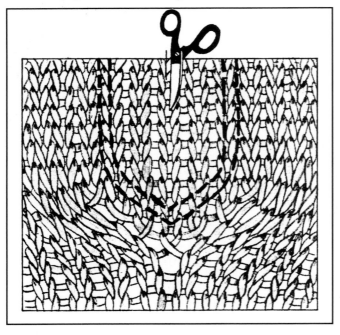

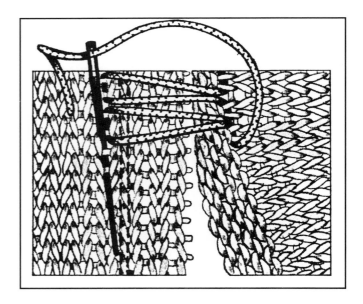

Vibrant Scarf, Gloves, and Socks Trio

▼ Materials

SCARF

Scheepjeswol Superwash Zermatt (50 g) 5 balls Red and 1 ball White

SOCKS

Scheepjeswol Superwash Zermatt (50 g) 3 balls Red and 2 balls White, Scheepjeswol Invicta Extra (50 g), 1 ball each Red and White

GLOVES

Neveda Skol 1 ball each Red and White

NEEDLES

Double-pointed U.S. size 3 and 5 (3 and 3.75 mm) knitting needles for Scarf and Socks, double-pointed U.S. size 2 and 3 (2.5 and 3 mm) knitting needles for Gloves

▼ Gauge

U.S. size 5 (3.75) needles in St st in Superwash Zermatt: 4" (10 cm) = 20 sts x 25 rows.

U. S. size 3 (3mm) needles in St st in Skol: 4" (10 cm) = 26 sts x 30 rows

To save time, take time to check gauge!

▼ Directions

SCARF

With red, cast on 80 sts and work 3 rounds of St st, then work in rounds of fairisle St st by foll chart. Carry unused yarn loosely across wrong side of work. Mark the beg of round. Work until piece measures 48" (120 cm) from beg, end with 3 rounds of red. Bind off. Thread a strand through end sts and gather tightly. Make 2 red pompoms 3-1/4" (8 cm) in diameter and sew to each end of scarf.

SOCKS

LEFT SOCK: With smaller size needle and Superwash Zermatt red, cast on 46 sts and work 1-1/4" (4 cm) in 1/1 ribbing. Mark beg of round. Knit 1 round, inc 14 sts evenly spaced around = 60 sts.

Change to larger size needles, work in fairisle St st by foll chart. Carry unused yarn loosely across back of work. After 33 rounds above ribbing = 6-1/4" (16 cm) from beg, end with 1 knit round. On the foll round, beg dec as foll: 15 sts in pat, k2 tog, k1, sl 1, k1, psso, work to end of round. Work these decs every 7th round 5 times, working the dec above the previous ones with the k1 between decs as the center back. After the last dec round, work the rem 50 sts for a total length of 14" (35 cm), end with 2 rounds in red. Shape heel: Work heel over the first 25 sts of round. With smaller size needle and 1 strand each of Invicta Extra, work back and forth in St st. After 17 rows, the last row is on the right side of work. Row 1: P14, p2 tog, p1, turn. Row 2: Sl 1, k4, k2 tog, k1, turn. Row 3: Sl 1, purl to 1 st before turning st, p2 tog, p1, turn. Row 4: Sl 1, knit to 1 st before turn, k2 tog, k1, turn. Work in this way until all sts are worked and the last row is on right side. With Zermatt, pick up 9 sts from side of heel, pick up 25 sts from top of foot, pick up 9 sts from side of heel and pick up sts from heel. Work in rounds of fairisle St st as above. On the foll round, dec as foll: Work the top of the foot sts, k1, sl 1, k1, psso, work the sts of the sole to the last 3 sts, k2 tog, k1. Work these dec every 3rd row until the sole and top of the foot have 25 sts each. Work these 50 sts until foot measures 7" (18 cm) from heel, end with 2 rounds of red. Change to 1 strand each of Invicta Extra and smaller size needle and work toe. Beg with 2nd round, dec as foll: K1, sl 1, k1, psso, work sole sts to last 3 sts, k2 tog, k2, sl 1, k1, psso, work top sts to last 3 sts, k2 tog, k1. Rep these dec every 2nd round until 18 sts rem. Knit the top sts and sole sts together. Work right sock same as left sock, but work heel over last 25 sts instead of first 25 sts.

GLOVES

With larger size needles and red, cast on 48 sts, work 4 rounds in St st, marking the beg of the round. Change to smaller size needle and work 4 rounds of 1/1 ribbing, dec 8 sts evenly spaced across first round = 40 sts. Knit 1 round, inc 8 sts evenly spaced = 48 sts. Change to larger size needles and work by foll chart for hand over 26 sts from point A to X and chart for thumb from X to Y, then foll chart for hand over 21 sts from Y to B. On the 5th round, shape thumb as foll: Work from A to X, then X to Y. With red, k1 in back of strand between sts, then work Y to B. Inc in this manner foll chart, on every 2nd round inc 2 sts. After the last inc, the thumb is 17 sts wide. Work to point C on both charts. On the foll round, work from A to X, place 17 sts of thumb on a stitch holder and cast on 3 sts in their place, then work from Y to B. Work 50 sts foll the chart to point D = 4-1/4" (11 cm) from the border. Place finger sts on holders by foll chart. Pick up 12 sts for little finger, cast on 3 sts at ring finger edge and work 15 sts in red in St st until finger measures 2-1/4" (5.5 cm) and shape top. On foll round, k2 tog around. Knit 1 round, then k2 tog. Break yarn and thread through rem sts and fasten off. Pick up 12 sts for ring finger and cast on 3 sts at middle finger edge and pick up 2 sts from little finger edge. Work these 17 sts for ring finger until finger measures 2-3/4" (7 cm), then shape top as before. Pick up 12 sts for middle finger, cast on 3 sts at index finger edge and pick up 3 sts from ring finger edge. Work these 18 sts for 3-1/4" (8 cm), then shape top. Pick up 14 sts for index finger, pick up 3 sts at middle finger edge and work these 17 sts until piece measures 2-1/2" (6.5 cm), then shape top as before. Pick up 17 sts of thumb and pick up 3 sts at hand edge and work these 20 sts until piece measures 2 1/2" (6.5 cm) and shape top as before. Work left hand the same, rev shapings.

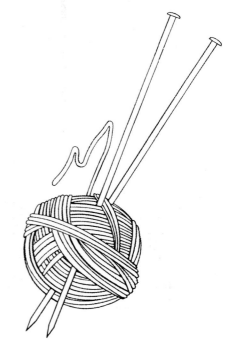

KEY TO CHART

⬤ = Red

☐ = White

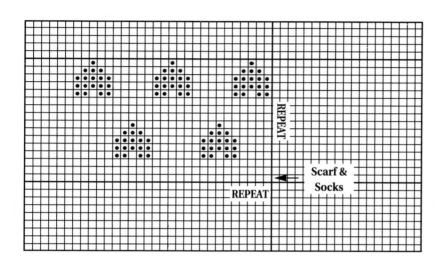

REPEAT

Scarf &
Socks

REPEAT

CHART for Thumb

CHART for Hand

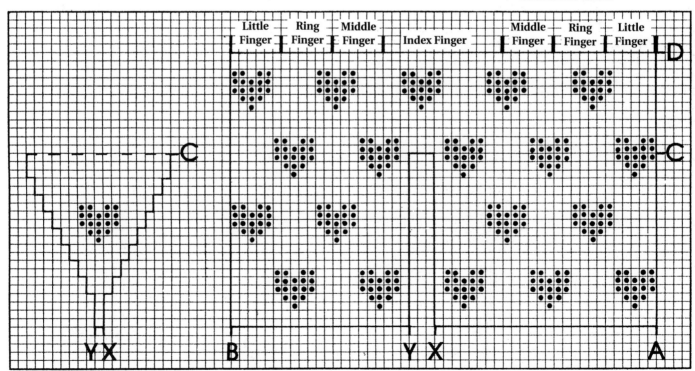

Fun and Funky Gloves

▼ Materials

COLORED FINGERS
Scheepjeswol Invicta Extra (50 g) 1 ball each of 7 colors of your choice

EYELET GLOVE
Scheepjeswol Invicta Extra (50 g) 1 ball each Yellow and Pink, elastic

PINK GLOVE
Scheepjeswol Invicta Extra (50 g) 1 ball each Purple and Pink

JACQUARD GLOVE
Scheepjeswol Invicta Extra (50 g) 2 balls MC, small amounts of CC

ALL GLOVES
U.S. size 1 and 2 (2 and 2.5 mm) double-pointed knitting needles

▼ Gauge

U.S. size 2 (2.5 mm) needles in St st: 2" (5 cm) = 16 sts x 22 rows.

To save time, take time to check gauge!

▼ Directions

FINGERS: Use these directions for all gloves. Work the indicated sts for the first finger in rounds, cast on sts between the first finger and the next

and work to indicated measurement. Shape Top: Each finger may have a different number of sts. These directions work for fingers which have 16, 17, 18, 19, 20, 21, 22, 23 and 24 sts. After the last round, break yarn and thread through rem 5 sts and fasten off.

16 st finger: Round 1: K2 tog, k14. Round 2: K15. Round 3: *K2 tog, k1*, rep * to * 5 times. Round 4: K2 tog 5 times. 17 sts finger: Round 1: K2 tog, k8, k2 tog, k5. Round 2: K15. Round 3: *K2 tog, k1*, rep * to * 5 times. Round 4: K2 tog 5 times. 18 st finger: Round 1: K2 tog, k5, k2 tog, k2, k2 tog, k5. Round 2: K15. Round 3: *K2 tog, k1*, rep * to * 5 times. Round 4: K2 tog 5 times. 19 st finger: Round 1: *K2 tog, k2*, rep * to * 3 times, k2 tog, k5. Round 2: K15. Round 3: *K2 tog, k1*, rep * to * 5 times. Round 4: K2 tog 5 times. 20 st finger: Round 1: *K2 tog, k2*, rep * to * 5 times. Round 2: K15. Round 3: *K2 tog, k1*, rep * to * 5 times. Round 4: K2 tog 5 times. 21 st finger: Round 1: K2 tog, k19. Round 2: *K2 tog, k2*, rep * to * 5 times. Round 3: K15. Round 4: *K2 tog, k1*, rep * to * 5 times. Round 5: K2 tog 5 times. 22 st finger: Round 1: K2 tog, k11, k2 tog, k7. Round 2: *K2 tog, k2*, rep * to * 5 times. Round 3: K15. Round 4: *K2 tog, k1*, rep * to * 5 times. Round 5: K2 tog 5 times. 23 st finger: Round 1: K2 tog, k7, k2 tog, k3, k2 tog, k7. Round 2: *K2 tog, k2*, rep * to * 5 times. Round 3: K15. Round 4: *K2 tog, k1*, rep * to * 5 times. Round 5: K2 tog 5 times. 24 st finger: Round 1: *K2 tog, k3*, rep * to * 3 times, k2 tog, k7. Round 2: *K2 tog, k2, rep * to * 5 times. Round 3: K15. Round 4: *K2 tog, k1*, rep * to * 5 times. Round 5: K2 tog 5 times.

GLOVE WITH COLORED FINGER

LEFT HAND: With smaller size needles and border color, cast on 48 (52) sts

and work 1-1/4" (3 cm) in 2/2 ribbing, inc 10 (12) sts evenly spaced around last round = 58 (64) sts.

Change to larger size needles and hand color and work 3 rounds in St st. Beg thumb: work 27 (30) sts in St st (palm), inc 1 in the strand between sts, k1 (foll thumb chart), k2 in St st, inc 1 = thumb, then 29 (32) sts of St st for top. Rep these incs on every 3rd round 8 (9) times. Between the inc you will have 2 sts. After the last inc, you will have 20 (22) sts for the thumb. Work 2 rounds. On the foll round, place 20 (22) sts for the thumb on a holder and cast on 2 sts in their place. Work 58 (64) sts until piece measures 4-1/2" (5") - 11.5 (12.5) cm from the top of the border. Work fingers as foll: place the first 7 (8) sts and the last 7 (8) sts of the round on a holder for the little finger, place 7 (8) sts from top of hand and palm of hand on a holder for ring finger, place 7 (8) sts from top of hand and palm of hand on a holder for middle finger, place rem 16 sts for the index finger. Work each finger in a different color. Pick up the little finger sts, casting on 3 (2) sts = 17 (18) sts and work in rounds in St st until finger measures 1/8" (.5 cm) from desired length and shape top. Pick up ring finger sts and pick up 3 (2) sts between the little finger and cast on 3(4) sts between the middle finger = 20 (21) sts. Work each finger same as little finger. Pick up the middle finger sts and pick up 3 (2) sts between the ring finger and cast on 3 sts between the index finger = 20 (21) sts. Pick up sts for index sts and cast on 3 (4) sts between the middle finger = 19 (20) sts. Pick up 20 (22) sts for thumb and cast on 2 sts and work over 22 (24) sts as on little finger.

RIGHT HAND: Work same as left hand,

working thumb on other side. Beg the thumb as foll: Work 29 (32) sts in St st = top, inc 1, work 2 sts in St st, inc 1 = thumb, work 27 (30) sts in St st = palm. Work border and finger in the same colors as on right hand and a different color for the hand.

EYELET GLOVES

LEFT HAND: With larger size needles and pink, cast on 108 sts and knit 1 round, change to yellow, then work 1/4" (1 cm) in 1/1 ribbing. Mark beg of round. On the foll round, dec 64 (60) sts by knitting 2 sts tog 24 (36) times and k3 tog 20 (12) times = 44 (48) sts on smaller size needles. Work as foll: Round 1: *K2 tog, yo*, rep * to *. Rounds 2 to 6: *K1, p1*, rep * to *. Round 7: *K2 tog, yo*, rep * to *. Round 8: Knit. Round 9: Knit, inc 10 sts evenly

CHART for Eyelet

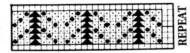

KEY TO CHART

· = K1

● = Yo

▲ = S1, k2 tog, Psso

spaced around = 54 (58) sts. Change to larger size needles, work in eyelet st foll chart, k2 (3). Round 10: K29 (32), 23 sts in eyelet foll chart, k2 (3). Round 11 and all odd rounds: Knit. Round 12: Like round 10. Round 14: Beg inc for thumb. Work 25 (27) sts, yo, k4, yo, k2 (3), 23 sts in eyelet st, k2 (3). Round 16: K25 (27), yo, k4, yo, k2 (3), 23 sts in eyelet, k2 (3). Round 18: K25 (27) sts, yo, k2 tog, k2, k2 tog, yo, k2 (3), 23 sts in

eyelet st, k2 (3). In this round, do not inc for thumb. Round 20: K25 (27), yo, k6, yo, k2 (3), 23 sts of eyelet st, k2 (3). In this round, inc 2 sts for thumb. Rep the 18th to the 21st rounds 5 (6) times. After each inc the thumb is 2 sts wider. After the last rep there will be 18 (20) sts between the eyelets. Knit 1 round. Place the 18 (20) sts for thumb plus inc 1 st at each edge on a holder and cast on 2 sts in place of thumb sts = 54 (58) sts. Work as foll: k29 (32) sts, 23 sts in eyelet pat, k2 (3). Work until piece measures 4" (5") - 11.5 (12.5) cm above the border, then shape fingers. Place the first and last 6 (7) sts on a holder for little finger, place 7 sts from top and palm for the ring finger and the middle finger and place the last 14 (16) sts for the index finger. Pick up the little finger sts, cast on 4 (3) sts between ring finger and work to 1/8" (.5 cm) from desired length of finger and shape top as above. Pick up ring finger sts and cast on 3 sts between the little finger and cast on 2 (3) sts between the middle finger = 19 (20) sts and work as before. Pick up middle finger sts, pick up 2 (3) sts from ring finger and cast on 3 sts between index finger = 19 (20) sts and work as before. Pick up index finger and pick up 4 (3) sts between the middle finger = 18 (19) sts and work as before. Pick up 20 (22) sts from the thumb and 2 (3) sts between the hand = 22 (24) sts and work as before.

RIGHT HAND: Work same as left hand, rev placement of thumb. Thread elastic at wrist.

PINK GLOVES

Pattern stitch: Multiple of 6. Round 1 through 3: With MC, knit. Round 4: *K4 with MC, k2 with CC*, rep * to *. Round 5: *K4 with MC, p2 with CC*, rep * to *. Rounds 6 through 8: Knit with MC. Round 9: *K1 with MC, k2 with CC, k3

with MC*, rep * to *. Round 10: *K1 with MC, p2 with CC, k3 with MC*, rep * to *. Always rep these 10 rounds.

LEFT HAND: With larger size needles and CC, cast on 58 (64) sts and work 1-1/2" (4 cm) in St st, marking beg of round. With MC, work 2 rounds in St st, dec 13 (14) sts on first round. Inc 9 (10) sts on foll round as foll: *K4 with MC, with CC, k1 in back and front strand of foll st*, rep * to * 9 (10) times = 54 (60) sts. Work the foll round in pat st, beg with the 5th round. Work 7 rounds above the border, inc for thumb as foll: work 25 (28) sts in pat st = palm, inc 1 in strand between sts, 2 sts in pat st, inc 1 between sts = thumb, 27 (30) sts in pat st = top of hand. Rep these inc 7 (8) times on every 3rd round. After the last inc, there will be 18 (20) sts for the thumb. Work 2 rounds. Place 18 (20) sts for thumb on a holder and cast on 2 sts in place of them = 54 (60) sts. Work in pat st until piece measures 4" (5") - 11.5 (12.5) cm above border ending with first or 2nd round of pat st in MC. For fingers, place first and last 6 (7) sts on a holder for little finger, place 7 sts of top and palm on a holder, place 7 (8) sts of top and palm on a holder and place last 14 (16) sts on holder. Work in rounds of pat st, staggering the 1 st dots. Pick up the little finger sts, cast on 4 (3) sts between the ring finger = 16 (17) sts and work to 1/4" (1 cm) less than desired length. Change to CC and work in St st for 2 rounds, then shape top as above. Pick up ring finger sts and pick up 3 sts between little finger and 2 (3) sts between middle finger = 19 (20) sts. Work as before. Pick up sts of middle finger, pick up 3 sts between ring finger and cast on 3 (2) sts between index = 19 (20) sts and work as before. Pick up index finger sts, pick up 4 (3) sts between middle finger = 18

(19) sts and work as before. Pick up 18 (20) sts from thumb and pick up 3 sts at hand = 21 (23) sts and work as before.

Right hand is worked the same, rev placement of thumb. Fold the border in half to inside and slip stitch in place. Thread elastic at wrist.

FAIRISLE GLOVES

LEFT HAND: The top and bottom are worked in different motifs, using one main color and as many contrasting colors as you desire. With smaller size needles and CC, cast on 52 (56) sts and work 3 rounds of 2/2 ribbing with 1 color, alternating with 2 rounds of MC. Mark beg of round. When ribbing measures 1-1/2" (4 cm), end with 1 round of MC. Inc 10 (18) sts evenly spaced around = 62 (74) sts and 1 round of MC. Change to larger size needles and work in fairisle St st foll chart 1 (2). Work the first round as foll: *1 st MC, 1 st CC*, rep * to * 15 (18) times, then **1 st MC, 5 sts CC**, rep ** to ** 5 (6) times, 1 st MC, 5 sts CC. Work 2 rounds by foll chart. Change CC and foll the chart. Beg the inc for thumb as foll: Round 4: 31 (37) sts in fairisle = palm, inc 1 st in the strand between sts, 1 st in pat, inc 1 = thumb, work 30 (36) sts = top. Work thumb sts in pat foll chart 3. The lower 3 sts on chart 3 are the same sts as the 3 sts between A and B on chart 1 (2). Foll the chart, changing the contrasting colors every 3 rounds. Between the inc, you have 2 more sts. After the last inc, you will have 25 (28) rounds in fairisle and 19 (21) sts on thumb. Work 2 rounds foll the chart, then place thumb sts on a holder and cast on 3 sts in their place. Work 62 (74) sts to a height of 4"

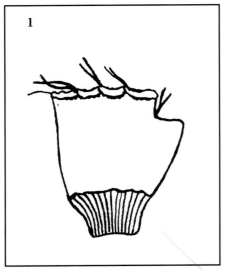

For each finger and thumb, place sts on holders as in photo.

(4-1/2") - 10.5 (11.5) cm above ribbing. End with 1 round of MC. Work fingers as foll: Place the first and last 7 (9) sts on a holder for the little finger, place next 8 (9) sts on top and palm on a holder for ring finger, place next 8 (9) sts on top and palm on a holder for middle finger, place last 16 (20) sts on a holder for index finger. With MC pick up finger sts and work charts 4, 5, 6, 7, 8, 9 or 10. Pick up little finger sts and cast on 4 (2) sts between ring finger and work 18 (20) sts to 1/8" (.5 cm) of desired length. Change to CC and shape top as above. Pick up ring finger sts and pick up 2 sts from little finger and cast on 2 sts between middle finger = 20 (22) sts. Work as above. Pick up sts of middle finger and pick up 2 sts between ring finger and cast on 2 sts between index finger = 20 (22) sts and work as above. Pick up index finger sts and pick up 3 (1) st between middle finger = 19 (21) sts and work as above. Pick up thumb sts and pick up 3 sts at hand edge = 22 (24) sts and work as above. Work right hand by rev placement of thumb and changing colors for fairisle motifs on fingers.

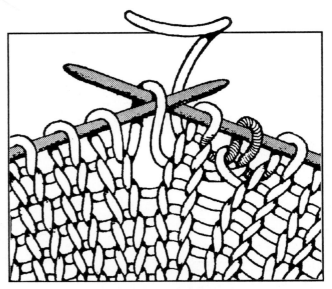

Inc in the strand between sts.

CHARTS for Jacquard Gloves

CHART 1 for Left Hand, Small Size

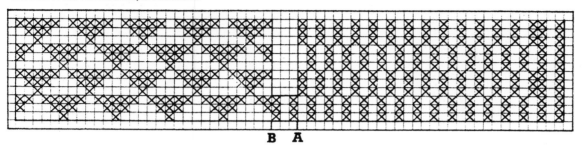

B A

CHART 2 for Left Hand, Large Size

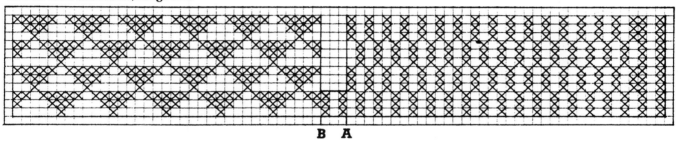

B A

CHART 3 for Thumb, Both Sizes

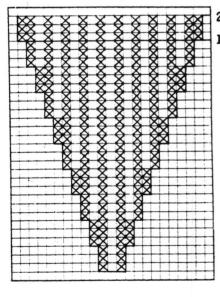

2
1

CHART 4 for Finger

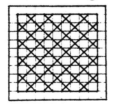

CHART 5 for Finger

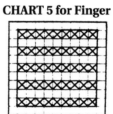

CHART 6 for Finger

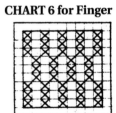

CHART 7 for Finger

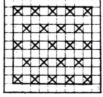

CHART 8 for Finger

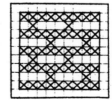

CHART 9 for Finger

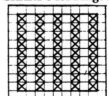

CHART 10 for Finger

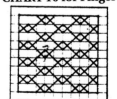

☒ = Gray - MC

☐ = Contrasting colors

Winter White Gloves and Scarf

▼ Materials

Neveda Skol (50 g) 1 ball Ecru for mittens; Scheepjeswol Superwash Zermatt (50 g) 11 balls Ecru for scarf; double-pointed needles U.S. size 2 and 3 (2.5 and 3 mm), U.S. size 5 (3.75 mm) needles

▼ Gauge

U.S. size 3 (3 mm) needles in St st: 4" (10 cm) = 25 sts x 34 rows.

U.S. size 3 (3 mm) needles in sand st: 4" (10 cm) = 25 sts x 30 rows.

U.S. size 5 (3.75 mm) needles in sand st: 4" (10 cm) = 18 sts x 26 rows.

U.S. size 5 (3.75 mm) needles in St st: 4" (10 cm) = 20 sts x 26 rows.

To save time, take time to check gauge!

▼ Stitches Used

Sand stitch:
Worked in rounds.

Round 1: Knit.

Round 2: *P1, k1*, rep * to * around.

Always rep these 2 rounds.

Sand stitch:
Worked in rows.

Row 1 and all odd rows (wrong side of work): *K1, p1*, rep * to *.

Row 2 and all even rows: Knit.

Always rep these 2 rows.

Left Cable:
Rows 1, 3, 5 and 7 (wrong side of work): Purl.

Row 2, 4 and 6: Knit.

Row 8: Slip 3 sts onto cable needle and hold at front of work, k3, k3 from cable needle.

Always rep these 8 rows.

▼ Directions

GLOVES

RIGHT GLOVE: With smaller size double pointed needles, cast on 48 sts and work 1/2" (1.5 cm) in 1/1 ribbing. Mark the first st of the round and beg the round with p1.

Change to larger size double pointed needles and work in sand st until piece measures 3-1/4" (8 cm) from beg. Work 4 rounds as foll: 27 sts of sand st for the top of the hand, inc 1 by k1 in the back of strand between the next 2 sts, k1, inc 1 (these 3 sts are the beginning of the thumb), work rem 20 sts for palm. On every 2nd round, inc 1 st at each edge of thumb sts 7 times. Always knit the thumb sts. After all incs, there will be 17 sts for the thumb. Work 3 rounds even. On the foll round, work 27 sts in sand st, place 17 sts of the thumb on a holder, cast on 3 sts between the top and palm, work 20 sts in sand st = 50 sts. Work even for 2" (5 cm) measured from holder. Knit 1 round.

FINGERS: Place the first and last 6 sts of round on holder for the little finger. Place the next 6 sts on top and palm on holder for ring finger, place the foll 6 sts on top and palm on holder for middle finger and place the last 14 sts on holder for index finger. Pick up the little finger sts on larger size double pointed needles, cast on 3 sts at ring finger edge (= 15 sts) and work 2-1/2" (6 cm) in St st. On the foll round, k2 tog around. Knit 1 round. On the foll round, k2 tog around. Break yarn and thread through all sts and fasten off. Pick up 12 sts of ring finger, pick up 2 sts at little finger and cast on 2 sts at middle finger edge (= 16 sts) and work in the same way for 2-3/4" (7 cm). Work the top the same as little finger. Pick up middle finger sts, pick up 3 from the ring finger, cast on 3 sts at index edge (= 18 sts) and work 3-1/4" (8 cm) in St st. Form the top as before. Pick up index finger sts, pick up 3 sts at middle finger edge (= 17 sts) and work 2-3/4" (7 cm) in St st. Shape top as before. Pick up thumb sts, pick up 3 sts at hand edge (= 20 sts) for 2-1/2" (6.5 cm). Form the top as before.

LEFT GLOVE: Work same as right glove, rev position of thumb and fingers.

SCARF

With straight needles, cast on 110 sts, work wrong side as foll: 1 border st, *k1, p1*, rep * to * 4 times, k1, **p6 for cable, work * to * 7 times, k1**, work ** to ** 3 times, p6 for cable, rep * to * 4 times, k1, 1 border st. On foll rows, work the 15 sts between the 5 cables in sand st and beg and end row with 9 sts in sand st, 1 border st. When piece measures 64" (160 cm), bind off all sts.

Toys, Animals, and Dolls

▼ Materials

Mayflower Helarsgarn (large) or Cotton 8 (small) (50 g) small amounts of desired colors; U.S. size 3 (3 mm) knitting needles with Cotton 8 and 6 (4 mm) knitting needles with Helarsgarn, U.S. size B/1 (2.5 mm) or E/4 (3.5 mm) crochet hook

▼ Gauge

U.S. size 6 (4 mm) needles in St st: 4" (10 cm) = 20 sts x 29 rows.

U.S. size 3 (3 mm) needles in St st: 4" (10 cm) = 26 sts x 36 rows.

To save time, take time to check gauge!

▼ Directions

BODY AND HEAD: Begin with body: With smaller size needles, cast on 58 sts and work 5 rows in 1/1 ribbing.

Change to larger size needles, work in striped St st alternating 4 rows of each color for 5 stripes, then complete in St st. (Note: different stripes or simple geometric motifs may be knit if desired using the chart.) After 20 rows, divide work as foll: Place 15 sts on holder for half back, work 28 sts for front and place 15 sts for 2nd half back on holder. On front sts, 2 sts in from each edge, dec 1 st at each edge on first, 3rd, 7th and 11th row. Place sts on holder and work half backs the same, dec at armhole edge. Place 11 sts from half back, 20 sts from front and 11 sts from half back on same needle and work these 42 sts in 1/1 ribbing for 4 rows. K2 tog at center of first row = 41 sts. Bind off. Pick up 41 sts from wrong side of last row of St st in light beige for head. On rows 1 and 2, work 41 sts of St st so that the first row is the right side of work. Row 3: K10, inc 1 in the strand between the sts, k2, inc 1, k17, inc 1, k2, inc 1, k10. Row 4: P45. Row 5: K11, inc 1, k2, inc 1, k19, inc 1, k2, inc 1, k11 (4 sts inc) = 49 sts. Rows 6 to 8: 49 sts in St st. Row 9: Inc 4 above previous inc, beg with k12 and so on. Row 10: P53. Row 11: Knit across, shaping nose on center st: K1, p1, k1, turn, p3 tog, turn and k3 tog. Rows 12 to 14: Work 53 sts in St st. Row 15: K11, sl 1, k1, psso, k2, k2 tog, k19, sl 1, k1, psso, k2, k2 tog, k11. Rows 16 to 18: 49 sts in St st. Work 4 rows, dec 4 sts on the 19th and 21st row above previous dec. Row 23: K7, *sl 1, k1, psso*, work * to * twice, k2 tog twice, k11, work * to * twice, k2 tog twice, k7. Row 24: P33. Row 25: Dec 8 sts as in the 23rd row, but beg and end with k5. Row 26: P25. Row 27: Dec 8 sts as in the 23rd row, but beg and end with k3. Bind off the rem 17 sts.

SLEEVE: Beg at the top. With larger size needles and desired color, cast on 25 sts, work St st or in stripes if desired. Work 11 rows. Dec 1 st at each edge of every 4th row twice. End with 2 rows of 1/1 ribbing and bind off. With beige or desired color, pick up 21 sts from inside last row of St st so that the first row is right side of work row. Work 6 rows in St st. Row 7: K1, sl 1, k1, psso, k5, k2 tog, k1, sl 1, k1, psso, k5, k2 tog, k1. Row 8: P17. Row 9: Like row 7, but k3 instead of k5. Row 10: P13. Break yarn and thread through sts. Fasten off. Sew the hand and sleeve seam. Sew the sleeves to body. Sew the center back seam. Sew the collar seam and fold to outside. Sew top of head. Embroider eyes and mouth using photo as a guide.

HAIR: For the boy, cut strands 5-1/4" (13 cm) long. Fold each strand double and with a crochet hook, join to the head. Beg at the back of the head and join strands wherever desired. If you wish, cut the loops. For the girl: For braids, cut strands 14" (35 cm) long. Join the strands to the back of the head along the back seam. End 6 rows above the nose. Gather the strands together at the sides of the head and braid. Fasten the braid with yarn and trim ends. Make bangs same as boy's hair. Satin stitch along the part.

WITCH: With black, cast on 82 sts and knit 1 row on wrong side of work. Continue in St st, knitting the first row to form a ridge. Row 6: (right side of work): Knit the 12th and 13th sts tog. Continue in St st, dec on the 10th, 14th and 18th rows, dec above previous decs = 58 sts. Work to the 25th row and shape armholes as on puppets. Rejoin 42 sts for the neck and knit 1 row on the wrong side of the work, k2 tog at center of work = 41 sts. Change to beige yarn for head and work as on Boy and Girl Puppets for 10 rows. Rows 11 to 16: 53 sts in St st. Row 17: K11, sl 1, k1, psso, k2, k2 tog, k19, sl 1, k1, psso, k2, k2 tog, k11. Rows 18 to 20: 49 sts in St st. Row 21: K10, sl 1, k1, psso, k2, k2 tog, k17, sl 1, k1, psso, k2, k2 tog, k10 = 45 sts. Continue in black for hat. Purl 3 rows to form ring. On the foll right side of work row, k9, sl 1, k1, psso, k2, k2 tog, k15, sl 1, k1, psso, k2, k2 tog, k9. Purl the foll row. Rep these 2 rows until 13 sts rem, dec at each edge of the 2 knit sts. Foll row: K1, sl 1, k1, psso, k2, sl 1, k2 tog, psso, k2, k2 tog, k1. P9 on wrong side. Last row: K1, k2 tog, sl 1, k2 tog, psso, k2 tog, k1. Break yarn and thread through rem 5 sts. Fasten off. Leave end to sew up back of hat.

BRIM: Pick up 45 sts from the ridge at the beg of the hat. In black, purl 1 row. Row 2: Inc after every 4th st = 56 sts. Row 3: P56. Row 4: K2, inc 1, *k5, inc 1*, rep * to *. Row 5: P67. Row 6: *K6, inc 1*, rep * to *. Row 7: P78. Row 8: Knit and bind off.

SLEEVE: With black, cast on 25 sts and work 10 sts in St st. Dec 1 st at each edge of every 4th row twice. Knit 3 rows. Change to beige. Rows 1 to 4: 21 sts in St st. Row 5: K1, sl 1, k1, psso, k5, k2 tog, k1, sl 1, k1, psso, k5, k2 tog, k1. Continue in St st, dec 4 sts on each right side row above previous dec until 9 sts rem. On foll right row (right side of work): K1, sl 1, k2 tog, psso, k1, sl 1, k2 tog, psso, k1. Break yarn and thread through rem sts. Fasten off. With black, pick up 21 sts from last row above hand and work 5 rows of garter st, inc 1 st after every 2nd st on the first row = 31 sts. Bind off loosely.

NOSE: With white, cast on 14 sts and work in St st. Purl the first row for wrong side of work. Work 5 rows. Row 6: K4, k2 tog, k2, sl 1, k1, psso, k4. Work these dec on every wrong side of row

until 8 sts rem. Purl these sts, break yarn and thread through sts. Leave a long end. Sew the underside of the nose to the face 9 rows above neck and stuff then sew nose. Embroider the mouth in black with 3 stem sts and make 1 duplicate stitch at mouth for fang. Sew body tog as on puppet. Make loops of hair under hat (see Boy and Girl Puppets).

KEY TO CHART

☒ = Yellow

☐ = Light Blue

· = Turquoise

CHART for Puppet Face

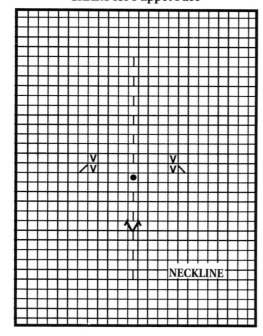

NECKLINE

CHART for Girl Puppet

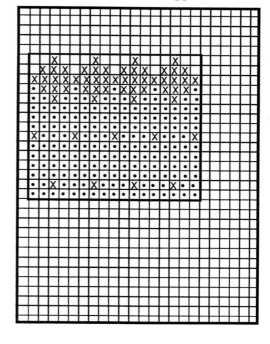

Bear Family

▼ Materials

Wool or cotton in desired color (brown
for head, hands and body, and desired
colors for stripes), doll eyes, black yarn
for embroidering nose and mouth,
stuffing

▼ Gauge

Depends on the thickness of the yarn
used. For example: U.S. size 2 (2.5 mm)
needles in sport weight yarn in garter
st: 4" (10 cm) = 24 sts x 48 rows. This
would give you a bear 14" (35 cm) in
height.

To save time, take time to check gauge!

▼ Directions

BODY: Beg at neck edge. With desired
color, cast on 18 sts and work 8 rows in
1/1 ribbing. Change to garter st. Cast
on 4 sts at each edge of foll row = 26 sts.

Knit 36 rows = 18 ridges. Note: Change
color every one or two ridges. Work 6
rows of 2/2 ribbing in desired color.
Change to pants color and work 6 rows
of 1/1 ribbing. Divide work in half and
join 2nd ball of yarn to last 13 sts. Work
20 rows of 1/1 ribbing. Change to
brown and work 8 rows in garter st for
paws. Dec 1 st at beg of every foll row
until 7 sts rem. Bind off. Make a 2nd
identical piece.

ARMS: Beg at top of arm. With desired
color, cast on 18 sts and work in striped
garter st as on body for 36 rows. Work 6
rows of 2/2 ribbing in desired color.

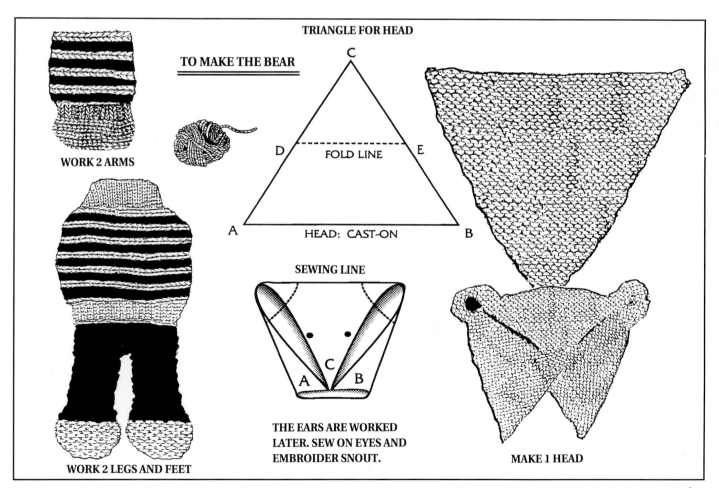

WORK 2 ARMS

TO MAKE THE BEAR

TRIANGLE FOR HEAD

C

D — FOLD LINE — E

A — HEAD: CAST-ON — B

SEWING LINE

A C B

THE EARS ARE WORKED
LATER. SEW ON EYES AND
EMBROIDER SNOUT.

WORK 2 LEGS AND FEET

MAKE 1 HEAD

Change to brown and work 4 rows of garter st. Dec 1 st at beg of foll rows until 12 sts rem. Bind off. Make a 2nd arm.

HEAD: Beg with the base of the triangle. Cast on 60 sts in brown and work in garter st. Rows 1 and 2: K 60. Row 3: K2 tog, work to the last 2 sts, k2 tog. Rows 4, 5, and 6: Knit. Row 7: Like row 3. Rep these 7 rows until 8 sts rem = 91 rows. Foll row: K2 tog, k4, k2 tog. Foll row: K6. Foll row: k2 tog, k2, k2 tog. Last row: k2 tog, k2 tog. Bind off.

FINISHING: Sew arm seams, leaving top open. Stuff arms. Sew shoulder seam of body. Sew leg and side seams, leaving opening at neck for stuffing. Stuff body. Fold the head triangle at line D-E with the point near the middle of the base. Sew the short seam A-B over a height of 2 ridges. Sew point C to A-B. Sew point A-B to neck edge over 2" (5 cm) of head - lower edge. Sew on the eyes 1" (2.5 cm) from the side seams and 1" (2.5 cm) from the fold line. Use the same strand of yarn to sew on the eyes so that they pull together slightly. Stuff head and sew to neck. Fold collar to outside. Embroider claws on paws in black yarn, making each st about 1" (2.5 cm) long. Make 3 sts. Embroider nose and mouth.

Chicken

▼ Materials

Mayflower Cotton 8 (50 g) 1 ball each Yellow, Orange, Green, and Blue; U.S. size 3 (3 mm) knitting needles; stuffing, 2 blue buttons for eyes

▼ Gauge

U.S. size 3 (3 mm) needles in St st: 2" (5 cm) = 13 sts x 18 rows.

To save time, take time to check gauge!

▼ Directions

HEAD: With orange, cast on 4 sts. Work entirely in St st, working shaping rows as foll: Row 1: K2 sts in every st by knitting in back and front strand of each st. Row 3: Like row 1 = 16 sts. Row 5: *K1, work 2 sts in every st*, rep * to * 24 sts. Row 9: *K2, work 2 sts in every st*, rep * to * = 32 sts. Row 13: Like row 9 = 42 sts, end with k2. Row 17: Work in yellow, like row 9 = 56 sts. Row 31: *K1, k2 tog*, rep * to * = 38 sts, end with k2. Row 35: Like row 31 = 26 sts, end with k2. Row 37: K2 sts tog across = 13 sts. Row 39: Like row 37 = 7 sts. Break yarn and thread through rem sts.

BODY: Cast on 8 sts in blue and work in St st working shaping rows as foll: Row 1: K2 sts in every st = 16 sts. Row 5: Like row 1 = 32 sts. Row 7: *K1, work 2 sts in 1 st*, rep * to * = 48 sts. Row 9: *K5, k2 sts in 1 st*, rep * to * = 56 sts.

Row 17: *K2, k2 tog*, rep * to * = 42 sts. Row 21: Continue in green, like row 17 = 32 sts, end with k2. Row 31: Like row 17 = 24 sts. Bind off on the 33rd row.

LEGS AND FEET: Cast on 4 sts in orange and work in St st. Inc 1 st at each edge of every 3rd, 7th, 9th and 11th row = 12 sts. After the 17th row, bind off all sts. Make 2 pieces for legs. For feet, cast on 12 sts in orange and work 6 rows in St st. Make 3 more pieces.

WINGS: Cast on 4 sts in yellow and work in St st. Row 1: Work 2 sts in each st = 8 sts. Inc 1 st at each edge of 3rd, 5th, 9th, 11th and 13th rows = 18 sts. After the 14th row, work 2 rows in green and bind off. Make a 2nd piece.

TAIL: Cast on 4 sts in yellow and work in St st. Row 1: Work 2 sts in each st = 8

sts. Inc 1 st at each edge of 3rd and 5th row = 12 sts. Bind off on the 7th row.

PANT LEGS: Cast on 18 sts in blue and work 2 rows in St st. Bind off loosely.

STRAPS: Cast on 20 sts in blue and knit 1 row. Bind off loosely. Make 2.

FINISHING: Sew the head seam, right sides together, leaving an opening to turn and stuff. Stuff head and sew closed. Sew center back seam of body, leaving an opening. Turn and stuff and sew closed. Sew on head to body. Sew pants in a ring. Sew the 2 parts of the feet together. Place pants over legs and sew to body. Sew side seams of wings and sew to body as shown in photo. Sew on straps, crossing at back. Stuff the tail and sew to back. Sew on blue buttons for eyes, spaced 16 sts apart. Make loops of yellow yarn for top of head.

▼ Materials

Mayflower Cotton 8 (50 g) 2 balls Beige, 1 ball each Pink, White, Blue, Yellow, and Dark Pink; U.S. size 2 (2.5 mm) knitting needles, U.S. size B/1 (2.5 mm) crochet hook; stuffing

▼ Gauge

U.S. size 2 (2.5 mm) needles in St st: 2" (5 cm) = 16 sts x 24 rows.

To save time, take time to check gauge!

▼ Directions

LEG: With pink, cast on 29 sts and work in St st as foll: Row 1: Purl = wrong side of work. Break yarn and continue in beige to row 32. Row 32: K11, sl 1, k1, psso, k3, k2 tog, k11 = 27 sts. Work 1 row. Row 34: K11, sl 1, k1, psso, k1, k2 tog, k11 = 25 sts. Work 5 rows. Row 40: K3, inc 1 st in the strand between sts, k19, inc 1, k3 = 27 sts. Work 1 row. Row 42: K3, inc 1, k21, inc 1, k3 = 29 sts. Work 8 rows. Row 50: K2, sl 1, k1, psso, k21, k2 tog, k2 = 27 sts. Work 3 rows. Row 54: K2, sl 1, k1, psso, k19, k2 tog, k2 = 25 sts. Work 1 row. Row 56: K2, sl 1, k1, psso, k17, k2 tog, k2 = 23 sts. Break yarn and work sock. Row 57: With white, work in St st. Row 58: P2, p2 tog, p15, p2 tog, p2 = 21 sts. Work 1 row. Row 60: K2, sl 1, k1, psso, k13, k2 tog, k2 = 19 sts. Break yarn and change to blue. Row 61: St st. Work heel over first and last 7 sts. (Center 5 sts are top of foot) Work first 7 sts, leave 12 sts unworked. Work 6 rows in St st, then work in short rows as foll: K4, turn, sl 1, p3, turn, k5, turn, sl 1, p4, turn, k6, turn, sl 1, p5, turn, k7, turn, sl 1, p6. Break yarn. Work on last 7 sts in the same way, rev shaping. Now work across all sts as foll: Row 1: Purl = wrong side of work, p7, p3 sts along side of heel, p5 for top of foot, purl 3 sts along other side of heel, p7 = 25 sts. Row 2: K8, k2 tog, k5, sl 1, k1, psso, k8 = 23 sts. Row 3 and all odd rows: Purl. Row 4: K7, k2 tog, k5, sl 1, k1, psso, k7 = 21 sts. Row 6: K6, k2 tog, k5, sl 1, k1, psso, k6 = 19 sts. Row 8: Knit. Row 10: K5, k2 tog, k5, sl 1, k1, psso, k5 = 17 sts. Row 12: K4, k2 tog, k5, sl 1, k1, psso, k4 = 15 sts. Row 14: K3, k2 tog, k5, sl 1, k1, psso, k3 = 13 sts. Row 15: Purl. Break yarn and thread through rem sts.

ARMS: With beige, cast on 18 sts and work in St st, working shaping rows as foll: Row 1: Purl = wrong side of work. Row 4: K3, inc 1, k12, inc 1, k3 = 20 sts. Row 8: K3, inc 1, k14, inc 1, k3 = 22 sts. Row 12: K3, inc 1, k16, inc 1, k3 = 24 sts. Row 28: K9, k2 tog, k2, sl 1, k1, psso, k9 = 22 sts. Row 32: K9, inc 1, k4, inc 1, k9 = 24 sts. Row 40: K2, sl 1, k1, psso, k16, k2 tog, k2 = 22 sts. Row 44: K2, sl 1, k1, psso, k14, k2 tog, k2 = 20 sts. Row 48: K2, sl 1, k1, psso, k12, k2 tog, k2 = 18 sts. Row 52: K2, sl 1, k1, psso, k10, k2 tog, k2 = 16 sts. Row 56: K2, sl 1, k1, psso, k8, k2 tog, k2 = 14 sts. Rows 57 to 59: St st = wrist. Row 60: K1, inc 1, k5, inc 1, k2, inc 1, k5, inc 1, k1 = 18 sts. The center 2 sts between incs, shape the thumb. Row 62: K8, inc 1, k2, inc 1, k8 = 20 sts. Row 64: K8, inc 1, k4, inc 1, k8 = 22 sts. Row 66: K8, inc 1, k6, inc 1, k8 = 24 sts. Row 68: K10, k2 tog, sl 1, k1, psso, k10 = 22 sts. Row 69: P9, p2 tog in back strand, p2 tog, p9 = 20 sts. Row 70: K8, k2 tog, sl 1, k1, psso, k8 = 18 sts. Row 71: P7, p2 tog in back of strand, p2, p7 = 16 sts. Rows 72 to 76: St st. K2 tog. Break yarn and thread through rem sts.

BODY: With pink, cast on 56 sts and work in St st as foll: 1 row in pink, *2 rows in white, 2 rows in pink*, rep * to * 3 times. Work in St st, working shaping rows as foll: Row 1: Purl = wrong side of work. Row 4: Inc 6 sts = 62 sts. Row 6: K16, inc 1, k30, inc 1, k16 = 64 sts. Row 8: K16, inc 1, k32, inc 1, k16 = 66 sts. Row 10: K17, inc 1, k32, inc 1, k17 = 68 sts. Change to beige, continue in St st. Row 24: K16, sl 1, k1, psso, k32, k2 tog, k16 = 66 sts. Row 26: K15, k2 tog, sl 1, k1, psso, k28, k2 tog, sl 1, k1, psso, k15 = 62 sts. Row 28: K1, sl 1, k1, psso, k11, k2 tog, sl 1, k1, psso, k11, p2 tog twice, k11, k2 tog, sl 1, k1, psso, k11, k2 tog, k1 = 54 sts. Row 30: K1, sl 1, k1, psso, k48, k2 tog, k1 = 52 sts. Rows 31 to 35: St st = waist. Row 36: K13, inc 1, k26, inc 1, k13 = 54 sts. Row 40: K14, inc 1, k26, inc 1, k14 = 56 sts. Row 44: K14, inc 1, k26, inc 1, k14 = 56 sts. Row 46: K14, inc 1, k28, inc 1, k14 = 58 sts. Row 48: K15, inc 1, k28, inc 1, k15 = 60 sts. Row 60: K14, sl 1, k2 tog, psso, k26, sl 1, k2 tog, psso, k14 = 56 sts. Row 62: K8, bind off 13 sts by knitting the 5th and 6th sts tog and the 8th and 9th sts tog, k14, bind off 13 sts as before, k8 = 30 sts. Row 63: P7, p2 tog, k12, p2 tog, p7 = 28 sts. Work to row 66. Bind off.

HEAD: With beige, cast on 28 sts and work in St st, working shaping rows as foll: Row 1: Purl = wrong side of work. Row 6: Work 2 sts in each st = 56 sts. Row 10: K14, inc 1, k1, inc 1, k26, inc 1, k1, inc 1, k14 = 60 sts. Row 12: K14, inc 1, k3, inc 1, k26, inc 1, k3, inc 1, k14 = 64 sts. Row 16: K15, inc 1, k3, inc 1, k28, inc 1, k3, inc 1, k15 = 68 sts. Row 20: K16, inc 1, k3, inc 1, k30, inc 1, k3, inc 1, k16 = 72 sts. Row 26: K35, p2 tog = nose, k35 = 71 sts. Row 32: K15, sl 1, k1, psso, k3, k2 tog, k27, sl 1, k1, psso, k3, k2 tog, k15 = 67 sts. Row 36: K14, sl 1, k1, psso, k3, k2 tog, k25, sl 1, k1, psso, k3, k2 tog, k14 = 63 sts. Row 40: K13, sl 1, k1, psso, k3, k2 tog k23, sl 1, k1, psso, k3, k2 tog, k13 = 59 sts. Row 44: K12, sl 1, k1, psso, k3, k2 tog, k21, sl 1, k1, psso, k3, k2 tog, k12 = 55 sts. Row 48: Knit every 3rd and 4th st tog = 42 sts. Row 50: Knit the 2nd and 3rd st tog = 28 sts. Row 52: K2 tog across = 14 sts. Row 53: Purl. Break yarn and thread through rem sts.

FINISHING: Sew back and lower seam of body. Sew shoulder seams and stuff body. Embroider the socks in white and the blue shoes as foll: Beg the embroidery in the 5th blue row from the sock, embroider over the center 3 sts of the top of the foot over 4 rows. Sew the sole of the shoe and the back seam. Sew the back seam of the leg and stuff. Sew the leg to body. Sew arms, first stuffing hands. Stuff the rest of the arms and sew to body so that the seam is at top. Embroider the head in half and whole duplicate st by foll chart. Embroider the mouth in dark pink, the cheeks in pink and the eyes in blue. The nose on the chart shows 2 sts but they are knit tog on the head. Embroider the eyes 7 or 8 sts apart. Sew back seam of head. Stuff head and gather sts at top. Stuff the neck and the body and sew seam, inserting head in neck. Cut strands of yellow yarn for hair 26" (65 cm) long. Sew hair on as shown in photo, knotting along hairline. Beg 11 rows above eyes over 13 sts. Back of head: Beg on the 10th row above neck over 18 sts. Sides: Attach the hair in a slanted line between the front and back. Gather the hair in a rubber band at top of head. Trim ponytail and attach short strands for bangs.

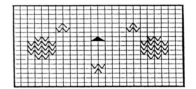

FINISHED MEASUREMENTS

Doll Man and Woman Height
8" (20 cm)

Doll Child Height
5-1/2" (14 cm)

▼ Materials

Mayflower Cotton 8 (50 g) 1 ball each
Ecru, Light Yellow, Yellow, Purple,
Beige, Brown, Light Blue, Blue, Dark
Blue, Green, Red, and Light Brown;
U.S. size 2 and 3 (2.5 and 3 mm)
knitting needles, U.S. size B/1 (2.5 mm)
crochet hook; 2 round buttons
for eyes and 1 wooden bead for nose
for each elf, stuffing, 5 small red
buttons, 4 small dark blue buttons,
2 yellow and 2 blue wooden balls,
1 buckle, pink pastel stick to
color cheeks

▼ Directions

Work pat 1 for the gnomes, pat 2 for
the women and pat 3 for the children.
Work in St st in desired colors.

PATTERN 1

Beg the body and the head at the top of
the head in desired color. Cast on 4 sts
and work in St st. Inc 1 st at each edge
of every 4th row 4 times = 12 sts. Row
17: *K2 in 1 st, k1*, rep * to * = 18 sts.
Rows 18 to 20: St st. Row 21: Like row
17 = 27 sts. Rows 22 to 24: St st. Row 25:
Like row 17 = 41 sts. Rows 26 to 31: St
st. Rows 32 to 36: Garter st. Row 37:
With beige, k31, turn, sl 1, p20, sl 1,
turn, knit to end of row. Row 38: Purl.
Row 39: Knit 33, turn, sl the first st, p24,
turn, sl 1, knit to end of row. Row 40:

Purl. Row 41: K35, turn, sl 1 the first st,
p28, turn, sl 1, knit to end of row. Rows
42 to 46: Work in St st. Row 47: K2 tog
across = 21 sts. Row 48: Purl. Row 49:
Knit in desired color for body. Row 50:
Purl. Row 51: *K1, work 2 sts in the foll
st*, rep * to * = 31 sts. Rows 52 to 60: St
st. Row 61: Continue in color for pants:
K2, inc 1 st in foll 2 sts, rep * to *
across = 41 sts. Rows 62 to 74: St st.
Row 75: In the first, 20th, 21st and last
st, work 2 sts = 45 sts. Row 76: Purl.
Row 77: Work 2 sts in the first, 22nd,
23rd and last st = 49 sts. Row 78: Purl.

Work legs as foll: Row 1: K23, bind off 3
sts, k23. Work each leg separately. Row
2: Work the first and last 2 sts tog = 21
sts. Row 3: Knit. Row 4: Like row 2 = 19
sts. Rows 5 and 6: St st. Row 7: Work in

desired color for shoes in garter st. Row
8: Knit. Row 9: *K1, k2 tog*, rep * to *
across = 13 sts. Row 10: Knit. Row 11:
Knit. Row 12: Purl. Row 13: *K1, work 2
sts in the foll st*, rep * to * = 19 sts. Row
14: Purl. Row 15: Work 3 sts in the 4th
and 5th sts = 23 sts. Row 16: Purl. Row
17: Work 3 sts in the 5th and 8th sts =
27 sts. Row 18: Purl. Row 19: Work 3 sts
in the 7th and 9th sts = 31 sts. Row 20:
Bind off the first 10 sts and work to end
of row. Row 21: Knit. Row 22: Purl. Row
23: K2 tog, k7, work 3 sts in the foll 2
sts, k8, k2 tog 4 times = 23 sts. Row 24:
Purl. Row 25: Bind off.

Work other leg in the same way from
row 2 to 14th. Row 15: Work 3 sts in the
15th and 16th sts = 23 sts. Row 16: Purl.
Row 17: Work 3 sts in the 16th and 19th

sts = 27 sts. Row 18: Purl. Row 19: Bind off 10 sts, k7, work 3 sts in the foll st, k1, work 3 sts in the foll st, k7 = 21 sts. Row 20 to 22: St st. Row 23: K2 tog, k8, work 3 sts in the foll 2 sts, k7, k2 tog = 23 sts. Row 24: Purl. Row 25: Bind off all sts.

EARS: With beige crochet hook, ch 2, 4 sc in the 2nd ch, turn, 2 sc in each sc, break yarn and fasten off. Make a 2nd ear.

ARMS: With beige, cast on 4 sts and work in St st. Rows 1 and 2: Work 2 sts in each st = 16 sts. Row 3: Inc 1 st at each edge = 18 sts. Rows 4 to 9: St st. Row 10: *P1, p2 tog*, rep * to * = 12 sts. Row 11: Work in the same color as body: *K1, work 2 sts in foll st*, rep * to * across = 18 sts. Rows 12 to 14: Garter st. Rows 15 to 23: St st. Rows 24 to 29: Dec 1 st at each edge. Row 30: Bind off rem 6 sts.

PATTERN 2

With hair color, cast on 3 sts and work in St st. Rows 1 and 2: Work 2 sts in each st = 12 sts. Continue by foll pattern 1, beg with the 17th row. Work to 34th row with hair color, then work the 32nd, 33rd and 34th rows in St st instead of garter st. Continue in beige, work the 35th and 36th rows in St st instead of garter st. Make ears and arms by foll pat 1.

PATTERN 3

With hat color, cast on 3 st and work in St st. Inc 1 st at each edge of every 2nd row 4 times = 11 sts. Row 9: *K1, work 2 sts in foll st*, rep * to * = 16 sts. Rows 10 to 12: St st. Row 13: Like row 9 = 24 sts. Rows 14 and 15: St st. Row 16: Knit.

Row 17: *K2, work 2 sts in foll st*, rep * to * = 32 sts. Row 18: Knit. Row 19: With beige, k24, turn, sl 1, p15, turn, sl 1, k1. Row 20: Purl. Row 21: K28, turn, sl 1, p23, turn, sl 1, knit to end of row. Rows 22 to 26: St st. Row 27: k2 tog across = 16 sts. Row 28: Purl. Row 29: Work in body color: *K1, work 2 sts in the foll st*, rep * to * = 24 sts. Rows 30 to 34: St st. Row 35: Work in pants color: *K2, work 2 sts in the foll st*, rep * to * = 32

sts. Rows 36 to 44: St st. Row 45: Work 2 sts in the first, 16th,17th and last st = 36 sts. Row 46: Purl. Row 47: Work 2 sts in the first, 17th, 18th and last st = 40 sts. Row 48: Purl. Then work legs as foll: Row 1: K2 tog, k15, bind off 2 sts, k2 tog, k15, k2 tog. Work each leg separately. Row 2: P2 tog, p13, p2 tog = 15 sts. Rows 3 and 4: St st. Row 5: Work in shoe color in garter st. Row 6: Knit. Row 7: *k2, k2 tog*, rep * to * = 12 sts.

Row 8: Knit. Rows 9 and 10: St st. Row 11: Work 3 sts in the 4th st from the crotch edge = 14 sts. Row 12: Purl. Row 13: Work 3 sts in the 5th st from the crotch edge = 16 sts. Row 14: Purl. Row 15: Work 3 sts in the 7th st from the crotch edge = 18 sts. Row 16: Purl. Row 17: Bind off all sts. Work the 2nd leg the same, rev shapings and beg with the 2nd row.

ARMS: With beige, cast on 4 sts and work in St st. Row 1: Work 2 sts in each st = 8 sts. Row 2: Purl. Row 3: Inc 1 st at each edge = 10 sts. Rows 4 and 6: St st. Row 7: Work in body color: *K2, k2 sts in foll st*, rep * to * = 13 sts. Rows 8 to 14: St st. Rows 15 to 18: Dec 1 st at each edge. Row 19: Bind off rem 5 sts.

FINISHING OF GNOME AND WOMAN: Fold the body and head piece right sides tog and sew back seam to crotch, leaving a 2" (5 cm) opening. Place the back and front of legs together and sew inseam to garter st ridge. For the woman, place the piece right sides together and sew. Sew the foot seams. Turn the body right side out. Fold the arms in half right sides tog and sew seam. Turn right side out. Make the nose as foll: Insert the ball in the head at the nose. Stitch with beige to hold in the nose. Stuff the body and sew opening closed. Stuff the arms. Attach a thread to top of one arm and thread through body to 2nd arm. Sew on arms. Thread a double strand through neck and gather. Sew on eyes to head 1/4" (1 cm) under the hat spaced 8 sts apart. When sewing eyes, join a strand between them through head so they are set in head. For the woman, stitch 3 eyelashes with brown. Embroider the mouth 2 rows below nose and 3 sts wide. Sew ears to sides

of head vertically under the hat. Crocheted hair: Attach to head. Ch 20, skip 1, 1 sc in the foll st. Work a row of hair and as many more as you desire in this way in the first and 2nd row under the hat and on the back side of the head. Make a beard in the same way. See photo.

FINISHING OF THE CHILDREN: Follow directions for adults. Sew on arms to body. Sew on eyes on the 4th row under the hair line, spaced 4 sts apart. Embroider the mouth between the 4th and 5th row from the neck over 2 sts. See photo.

WOMAN WITH KERCHIEF: Work in the foll colors: Light brown for hair, beige for the head, light yellow for body and legs, ecru for the shoes. Make hair on the front over the 4th row from hair line and along the back on the first and 4th row. See photo.

SKIRT: With light yellow, cast on 60 sts and knit 2 rows. Rows 3 to 20: St st. Row 21: *K1, k2 tog*, rep * to * = 40 sts. Row 22: Purl. Bind off. Sew back seam. Place skirt over body and under arms.

APRON: With blue, cast on 18 sts and knit 2 rows. Continue in St st, working 2 sts at each edge in garter st. Work 14 rows. Row 17: Cast on 18 sts at beg of row. Row 18: Cast on 18 sts at beg of row, *p1, p2 tog*, rep * to * 5 times, work 18 sts. Row 19: Bind off first 18 sts and k30. Row 20: Bind off first 18 sts, k2, p8, k2. Rows 21 to 24: K2, 8 sts in St st, k2. Rows 25 to 28: Garter st. Row 29: Bind off center 8 sts. Work the first and last 2 sts for 24 rows for straps. Bind off. Sew the straps to the waist of apron.

KERCHIEF: With red, cast on 42 sts and

knit 1 row. Continue in St st. Dec 1 st at each edge as foll: Right side: Sl 1, k1, psso, knit to last 2 sts, k2 tog. Purl wrong side. Rep these dec 19 times. Bind off rem 2 sts. With crochet hook and red, ch 30, then work 1 round of sc around slanted edges of kerchief, end with ch 30. Fasten off. Embroider dots spaced 3 sts and 3 rows apart. Stagger the dots, 1 dot blue, 1 dot yellow. Tie the kerchief under the chin with a bow. See photo.

WOMAN WITH SHAWL: Work in foll colors: Light yellow for hair, beige for the face, ecru for the body and pants, blue for the shoes. Embroider with light yellow over the back of the head as foll: Beg under the first row with light yellow, 3 sts above the left ear. Embroider over the back and end with 3 sts over the right ear. Embroider over 4 rows, but work 1 less st at each edge. Make a braid with light yellow: cut strands 10" (25 cm) long. Thread 2 strands through each of 6 embroidered sts at each side. Braid strands and wrap around head. See photo.

SKIRT: With ecru, cast on 19 sts and work in St st, working 2 sts at each edge in garter st: Work 2 rows in ecru, 2 rows in purple, 2 rows in ecru, 2 rows in blue*, rep * to * once. Bind off. Pick up 1 st from every st with purple along 1 long side and knit 4 rows. Bind off. Sew back seam, leaving 1-1/4" (3 cm) open at waistband. With crochet hook and purple ch 25 for the belt. Work 1 round of sc with purple along lower edge of skirt. Fasten off. Place on body and tie at back.

SHAWL: With purple, cast on 2 sts and work in St st. At each edge of every row, inc 1 st 25 times = 52 sts. Bind off. Make fringe along slanted edges. Sew ends to front of body.

WOMAN WITH RED SKIRT: Work in foll colors: Yellow for hair, beige for face, red for body and pants and blue for shoes. Sew tog as before. Thread an 8" (20 cm) long strand through the center st beginning on 7th row above hairline. Continue to attach strands to center back hairline. Work this way around head. Use ends to make a braid above each ear. Wrap braid and sew in place. With crochet hook and blue, ch 60, fasten off and tie around neck. See photo.

SKIRT: With red, cast on 44 sts and knit 2 rows. Continue in St st. Work 3 rows. Row 4: 1 border st, *1 st in blue, 2 sts in red*, rep * to *, end with 1 border st. Row 5: 1 border st, 1 st in red, *1 st in blue, 1 st in red, 1 st blue, 3 sts in red*, rep * to *, end with 1 border st. Rows 6 to 20: St st in red. Bind off all sts. With light yellow and blue, embroider motifs using photo as a guide. With crochet hook and blue, ch 30, then work 1 sc in every 2nd st on the top of the skirt. In the last sc, make a 30 st chain. Fasten off. Tie at back of body.

GNOME WITH YELLOW HAT: Work in foll colors: Yellow for hat, beige for face, purple for body, blue for pants and yellow for shoes. Embroider the hair in light brown. See photo. For bib overalls, with blue, cast on 14 sts for bib and work in St st, knitting first and last st of all rows. On the 5th row, work as foll: K1, sl 1, k1, psso, k8, k2 tog, k1. Bind off after 9th row. Straps: With blue, cast on 3 sts. Work 20 rows in St st. Bind off. Pocket: With blue, cast on 8 sts and work 8 rows in St st. Bind off. Sew pockets to pants, 2 sts from the center and 1 row under the top edge of pants. Sew on bib at the first row to pants. Sew straps in place. Sew 2 buttons to bib to hold on straps.

GNOME WITH GREEN HAT: Work in foll colors: Green for the hat, beige for the face. Work the first 8 rows of body in stripe pattern: *2 rows in blue, 2 rows in green*, rep * to *. Work pants in blue and shoes light blue. Sew together as before. Make hair in ecru along the front in the first row under the hat. Make beard in ecru in the 2nd and 3rd row under the mouth. Make a green tassel and sew to hat with a ch 8 tie. See photo.

Vest: With red, cast on 40 sts and work in seed st (*k1, p1*, rep * to * across). On all foll row, work opposite st. After 11 rows work as foll: Work 8 sts, bind off 2 sts, work 20 sts, bind off 2 sts, work 8 sts. Work each section separately. Work last 8 sts for front. At center edge, dec 1 st on every 3rd row until 4 sts rem. Work 1 row. Bind off. Work 2nd front the same. Work center 20 sts for back to same height as front. Bind off. Sew shoulder seam. Sew 2 buttons on right front.

GNOME WITH RED HAT: Work in foll colors: Red for hat, beige for face, blue for body, light blue for pants and red for shoes. Sew together as before. Sew a blue button to toe of each shoe. Make ecru hair. Make chain loops at chin for beard. See photo.

Vest: Worked from side to side. Beg at left sleeve. With red, cast on 24 sts and work 4 rows in garter st, then work in stripe pattern *2 rows in green, 2 rows in red*, rep * to *. After 9 rows, at each end, cast on 8 sts for the body. Work the first and last 2 sts in garter st. Work 12 rows in stripe pattern. On the 13th row, divide work in half and work each part separately. Work 26 rows of stripe pat at right edge for back, working 2 sts at each edge in garter st. Place sts on

holder. Work 2nd half for front. 2 sts in from neck edge on every 2nd row, dec 1 st 4 times. Work 3 rows in garter st. Bind off. Cast on 16 sts and work 3 rows in garter st, continue in stripe pat, working 2 sts at each edge in garter st. 2 sts in from neck edge of every 2nd row, inc 1 st 4 times. Join the sts of the back with the sts on the needle and work 6 rows. At each edge, bind off 8 sts. Work 4 rows, end with 4 rows in garter st with red. Bind off all sts. Sew side and sleeve seams.

GNOME WITH PURPLE HAT: Work in foll colors: Purple for hat, beige for face, light blue for body, red for pants and purple for shoes. Sew tog as above. Make hair with light yellow. Make a red tassel for hat.

Vest: With blue, cast on 40 sts and knit 2 rows, continue in St st, working 2 sts at each edge in garter st. Work 8 rows. Row 9: Work 8 sts, bind off 2 sts, work 20 sts, bind off 2 sts, work 8 sts, work first and last 8 sts for the front. Work first and last 2 sts in garter st. 2 sts in from each center edge of every 3rd row, dec 1 st 4 times. Work 1 row over rem 4 sts, bind off. Work center 20 sts in St st, with 2 sts at each edge in garter st and work same as front. Bind off. Sew shoulder seams. Sew 3 red buttons on right front.

GNOME WITH BROWN HAT: Work in foll colors: Brown for the hat, beige for the face. Work the first 12 rows of body in stripes: *2 rows in light blue, 2 rows in blue*, rep * to *, complete in brown and shoes in green. Sew tog as above. Make hair in light brown on the back of the head in the first row under the hat. Work straps as foll: With brown, cast on 3 sts and work 32 rows of garter st. Bind off. Sew these 3 sts left over right at the center of the back and centered on front. Thread brown thread through top of shoes for laces. For pocket, with brown, cast on 8 sts and work 8 rows of St st, 2 rows of garter st. Bind off. Sew to right back pants.

GNOME WITH RED BELT: Work in foll colors: Blue for hat, beige for face, yellow for body, brown for pants and blue for shoes. Sew tog as before. Vest: Work in blue as on gnome with purple hat. Belt: With red, cast on 3 sts and work 11" (28 cm) in garter st. Bind off. Sew on at waist.

GNOME WITH CHECKED SHIRT: Work in foll colors: Blue for hat, beige for face, work top of body in checks in St st: Rows 1 and 2: *2 st in blue, 2 sts in light blue*, rep * to *. Rows 3 and 4: *2 sts in light blue, 2 sts in blue*, rep * to *. Work these 4 rows twice, then work rows 1 and 2 once. Continue in brown and work shoes in beige. Sew tog as before. Embroider 3 strands of light brown for hair. Beg above right ear, embroider 1 st over ear, then work embroidery over 3 sts across back to top of foll ear. Embroider 1 st above ear. Fasten off.
Vest: With red, cast on 40 sts and knit 2 rows. Continue in St st, working 2 sts at each edge in garter st. Work 8 rows. Row 9: Work 8 sts, bind off 2 sts, work 20 sts, bind off 2 sts, work 8 sts. Work the first and last 8 sts for the front. 2 sts in from center edge on every 3rd row, dec 1 st 4 times. Work 1 row over rem 4 sts. Bind off. Work the center 20 sts in St st to the same height as the front. Bind off. Pick up 26 sts along each armhole and work 4 rows. Bind off. Sew shoulder seams.

CHILD WITH BLUE HAT: Work in foll colors: Blue for hat, then work 16 to 18

rows in red, beige for face, body and pants in striped pattern. *2 rows blue, 2 rows red*, rep * to *. Shoes are blue. Sew tog as above. Make loops for hair in light yellow. Place on first row under hat and all over back. See photo. Sew on yellow to hat.

CHILD WITH SKIRT: Work in foll colors: Light yellow for hair, beige for face, light blue for body, beige for legs, shoes in dark blue. Sew tog as above. Make hair on the first row of light yellow above face. Leave the center 7 sts hairless. Thread 1-1/4" (3 cm) long strands in each st. Gather hair at top of head and tie with bow and trim sides. See photo. Skirt: With light blue, cast on 40 sts and knit 2 rows, continue in stripe pat: *2 rows in dark blue, 2 rows in light blue* rep * to * for 8 rows. Row 9: *K3, k2 tog*, rep * to *. Bind off. Sew the back seam. Sew skirt to waist of body.

CHILD WITH RED HAT: Work in foll colors: Red for the hat, beige for the face, ecru for the body, green for the pants and blue for the shoes. Sew tog as above. Embroider the hair with a double strand of light yellow: Above an eye make short sts and along the back make long sts. Straps: With crochet hook and green, ch 20. Fasten off. Make a 2nd strap. Sew to top of pants 2 sts apart. Cross at back.

CHILD WITH GREEN HAT: Work in foll colors: Green for hat, work the 16th to 28th rows in red, beige for face, blue for body, red for pants and green for shoes. Sew tog as above. Embroider hair in light yellow as on child with red hat. Sew 2 dark blue buttons to top of pants. See photo.

Mice Sweaters

FINISHED MEASUREMENTS

Chest
9-1/2" (24 cm)

Length
3" (7.5 cm)

Sleeve Length
1-3/4" (4.5 cm)

▼ Materials

Mayflower Cotton 8 (50 g) Small amounts of Green and Pink or Yellow and Light Blue or Yellow and Gray; U.S. size 2 and 3 (2.5 and 3 mm) knitting needles; 2 buttons

▼ Gauge

U.S. size 3 (3 mm) needles in St st: 4" (10 cm) = 26 sts x 36 rows.

To save time, take time to check gauge!

▼ Stitches Used

STRIPE PATTERN A: In St st work *2 rows green, 4 rows pink*, rep * to *.

STRIPE PATTERN B: In St st work *2 rows yellow, 2 rows light blue*, rep * to *.

STRIPE PATTERN C: In St st work *4 rows yellow, 4 rows gray*, rep * to *.

▼ Directions

BACK: With smaller size needles and pink or light blue or gray, cast on 32 sts and work 1/4" (1 cm) in 1/1 ribbing. Purl 1 row on wrong side of work, inc 2 sts evenly spaced on row = 34 sts.

Change to larger size needles, work in striped St st A or B or C.

Bind off when piece measures 3" (7.5 cm) from beg, ending with a whole stripe.

FRONT: Beg front same as back.

When piece measures 2-1/2" (6.5 cm) from beg, bind off center 12 sts. Join second ball of yarn to second part and work at the same time. At each neck edge of every 2nd row, dec 1 st twice.

When piece measures 3" (7.5 cm) from beg, end with a whole stripe. Bind off rem 9 sts on each shoulder.

SLEEVE: With smaller size needles and pink or light blue or gray, cast on 24 sts, work 1/4" (1 cm) in 1/1 ribbing. Purl 1 row on wrong side of work, inc 2 sts on last row = 26 sts.

Change to larger size needles, work in striped St st A or B or C.

When piece measures 1-3/4" (4.5 cm) from beg, end with a whole stripe. Bind off.

FINISHING: Sew right shoulder seam. On the left front shoulder, make 2 loops for button clasps. With smaller size needles and pink or light blue or gray, pick up and knit 32 sts around neck. Work 3/4" (2 cm) in 1/1 ribbing. Bind off. Fold neckband in half to outside. Sew on buttons and tack the shoulder seam. Sew sleeves to side seams. Sew side and sleeve seams.

Santa Doll

▼ Materials

Mayflower Cotton 8 (50 g) 2 balls each Pink and White, 1 ball Red, small amount Dark Pink, 50 g of thick fluffy cotton yarn; U.S. size 2 (2.5 mm) knitting needles; 2 plastic eyes, stuffing, 1-1/4" (3 cm) diameter styrofoam ball, fabric glue

▼ Gauge

U.S. size 2 (2.5 mm) needles in St st: 4" (10 cm) = 28 sts x 40 rows.

To save time, take time to check gauge!

▼ Directions

BODY AND HEAD: With white, cast on 30 sts and work 2 rows in St st. Row 3: Work 2 sts in each st = 60 sts. Rows 4-6: St st. Row 7: *K1, k2 in foll st*, rep * to * = 90 sts. Rows 8-12: St st. Row 13: *K4, k2 in foll st, * rep * to * 9 times, k45 = 99 sts. Rows 14-34: St st. Row 35: *K4, k2 tog*, rep * to * 9 times, k45 = 90 sts. Rows 36 to 44, St st. Row 45: *K4, k2 tog*, rep * to * = 75 sts. Rows 46-48: St st. Row 49: *K3, k2 tog*, rep * to * = 60 sts. Rows 50-52: St st. Row 53: *K2, k2 tog*, rep * to * = 45 sts. Rows 54-58: St st. Row 59: Change to pink for head. Row 60: St st. Row 61: K2 in each st = 90 sts. Rows 62-96: St st. Row 97: *K4, k2 tog*, rep * to * = 75 sts. Rows 98-102: St st. Row 103: *K3, k2 tog*, rep * to * = 60 sts. Rows 104-108: St st. Row 109: *K2, k2 tog*, rep * to * = 45 sts. Rows 110-112: St st. Row 113: *K1, k2 tog*, rep * to * = 30 sts. Row 114: St st.

Row 115: K2 tog across. Break yarn and thread through rem sts. Fasten off.

ARMS: With pink, cast on 13 sts and work 2 rows in St st. Row 3: K2 in every st = 26 sts. Rows 4-8: St st. Row 9: *K2, k2 sts in foll st*, rep * to * 8 times total, k2 = 34 sts. Rows 10-11: St st. Rows 12-13: Cast on 4 sts at beg of each row for thumb = 42 sts. Rows 13-22: St st. Rows 23-24: Bind off first 6 sts of each row = 30 sts. Rows 25-26: St st. Row 27: Continue in white. After 38 rows, bind off all sts. Make a second arm.

LEGS: With red, cast on 40 sts and work in striped St st: *2 rows red, 2 rows white*, rep * to * to 6 times total, 2 rows red. Row 1: K17, work 2 sts in foll st, k4 = toe, k2 in foll st, k17 = 42 sts. Row 3: K18, k2 in foll st, k4, k2 in foll st, k18 = 44 sts. Row 4: St st. Row 5: K19, k2 in foll st, k4, k2 in foll st, k19 = 46 sts. Rows 6-8: St st. Row 9: K19, k2 tog, k4, k2 tog through back loop, k19 = 44 sts. Rows 10, 12, 14, 16: St st. Rows 11, 13, 15 and 17: Dec 2 sts as in row 9, working dec above previous dec. Rows 18-26: St st. Row 27: Continue in St st in white. Work to row 36. Bind off. Work second leg the same.

NOSE: With dark pink, cast on 8 sts and work 2 rows of St st. Rows 3, 5, 7, 9 and rows 18, 20 and 22: St st. Inc 1 st at each edge = 16 sts. Rows 4, 6 and 8: St st. Rows 10-16: St st. Rows 17, 19, 21 and 23: Dec 1 st at each edge = 8 sts. Work a total of 24 rows. Bind off. Thread a piece of yarn around outside edges of pieces and gather. Line with stuffing and insert styrofoam ball. Sew closed.

FINISHING: Embroider the head in dark pink foll the chart in duplicate st, beg on the 21st row of pink. Beg at point A on the 9th st from the right edge.

Embroider the 2nd cheek on opposite side. Between the 2 cheeks there are 17 sts. Sew the body and head seam, leaving a 2" (5 cm) opening. Stuff the piece and sew opening. Thread yarn through the last row of white and 4 rows below first row of pink and gather for neck. Sew arm seams and stuff. Sew opening of arms closed and sew to side seams, with thumb at top, 1/2" (1.5 cm) under the neck. Sew leg seams, leaving top open. Stuff and sew top of legs. Sew legs to body spaced 1/4" (1 cm) apart. Sew on nose between the cheeks. Sew on the eyes on the 36th row of pink. Sew on both eyes at the same time. Make a knot at one eye position and pull thread through to second eye position. Attach second eye and thread through to first eye position. Attach first eye. Thread through a few times, pulling thread tight and fasten off. Sew on eyebrows 3/4" (2 cm) above eyes using fluffy yarn. Make small loops 1/8" (.5 cm) and large loops 1-1/4" (3 cm) long.

Beard and hair: Around 4 fingers of your hand, wrap fluffy yarn for hair and beard. Sew on 2 rows of these loops for beard and 3 rows for hair. Sew on first row of beard 1-1/4" (3 cm) under nose, continuing up sides and back of head. Sew second row under the first row so beard looks thick. For mustache, cut 4" (10 cm) strands of yarn and sew at center under nose. Cut ends of loops and trim. Glue on stuffing material under mustache and beard to fluff out.

CHART for Cheek

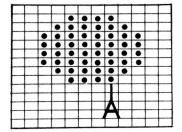

Country Bunnies

▼ Materials

LARGE BUNNY
Mayflower Helarsgarn (50 g) 2 balls
Gray, 1 ball White, black embroidery
floss, stuffing

Clothes
2 balls Red, Pink or Blue, 1 ball White;
U.S. size 4 and 6 (3.5 and 4 mm)
knitting needles, U.S. size F/5 (4 mm)
crochet hook; 1 round button for nose
and 2 flat buttons for eyes, ribbon, 2
buttons for pants, small amount of
white cotton

SMALL BUNNY
Mayflower Cotton 8 (50 g) 1 ball each
Gray and White; black embroidery
floss, stuffing

Clothes
1 ball Red or Blue and White; U.S. size 2
and 3 (2 and 3.5 mm) knitting needles,
U.S. size B/1 (2.5 mm) crochet hook; 1

round button for nose and 2 flat buttons for eyes, ribbon, 2 buttons for pants, small amount of white cotton

▼ Gauge

U.S. size 6 (4 mm) needles in St st with Helarsgarn: 4" (10 cm) = 19 sts x 16 rows.

U.S. size 3 (3 mm) needles in St st with Cotton 8: 4" (10 cm) = 26 sts x 30 rows.

To save time, take time to check gauge!

▼ Directions

Note: Both sizes are worked the same, but the large bunny is made with Helarsgarn and the small bunny is made with Cotton 8.

ARMS: With larger size needles and gray, cast on 20 sts and work 24 rows in St st. Inc 1 st at beg of every row 6 times, then work 2 rows even. Bind off 4 sts at beg of next 2 rows. Work 4 rows, then work as foll: Row 1: *K1, k2 tog*, rep * to * across. Row 2: P12. Row 3: *K1, k2 tog*, rep * to * across = 8 sts. Row 4: Purl and bind off. Make a 2nd arm.

LEGS: With larger size needles and gray, cast on 24 sts and work 26 rows in St st. Inc 1 st at center of row as foll: K11, work 2 sts in each of the next 2 sts, k11. Purl the foll row. On the foll row, k12, work 2 sts in each of the next 2 sts, k12. Continue to inc in this way until there are 32 sts on needle. Work 4 rows even, then bind off. Make a 2nd leg.

EARS: Make two in gray and two in white. Cast on 12 sts and work 24 rows even, then k2 tog across next 2 rows = 3 sts. K3 tog and fasten off.

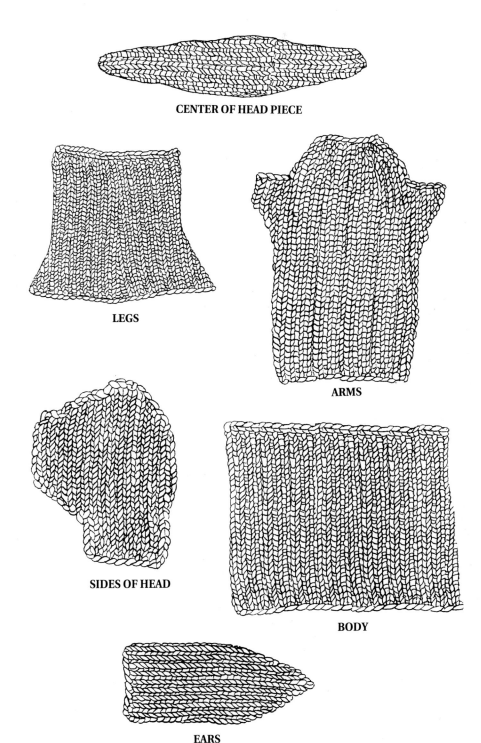

CENTER OF HEAD PIECE

LEGS

ARMS

SIDES OF HEAD

BODY

EARS

BODY: With larger size needles and gray, cast on 36 sts and work 26 rows in St st. Bind off.

SIDE OF HEAD: With larger size needles and gray, cast on 12 sts and work 8 rows in St st. At right edge of every row, inc 1 st 6 times = 18 sts. Work 10 rows even. At left edge of next 3 rows, k2 tog = 15 sts. Work 2 sts tog at beg of next 3 rows. Bind off 3 sts at beg of right side row and at the same time, p2 tog at beg of wrong side rows. Bind off rem 5 sts. Make a 2nd piece, rev shapings.

HEAD FRONT: With larger size needles and gray, cast on 1 st. Inc 1 st at each edge of every 2nd row twice. Work these 5 sts even for 5 rows. Inc 1 st at each edge of foll row = 7 sts. Work even for 5 rows. Inc 1 st at each edge of foll row = 9 sts. Work even for 17 rows. Dec 1 st at each edge of foll row. Work 3 rows. Dec 1 st at each edge of foll row. Work 5 rows. Dec 1 st at each edge of foll row. Work 4 rows even, then bind off.

FINISHING: Sew leg and arm seams. Stuff. Sew back and lower seams of the body. Stuff the body. Sew on arms and legs. Sew the center seams of the head, with the cast on edge at last inc of snout. Sew back seam of head. Stuff head and sew to body. Sew white and gray ears together and sew to head. Sew on eyes and nose and embroider the whiskers. Tack on ribbon.

CLOTHES
DRESS: With larger size needles and red or pink, cast on 91 sts and work in dotted St st as foll: Row 1: Knit. Row 2: Purl. Row 3: *3 sts in red or pink, 1 st in white*, rep * to *, end with 3 sts in red or pink. Rows 4 and 5: Like rows 1 and 2. Row 6: *1 st in red or pink, 1 st in white, 3 sts in red or pink*, rep * to *, end with 1 st in red or pink instead of 3 sts in red or pink. Rep these 6 rows. Work for a total of 28 rows. On the foll row, k2 tog = 46 sts. With smaller size needles, work 4 rows in 1/1 ribbing as foll: 13 sts for the half back, 20 sts for front and 13 sts for the 2nd back. Work each part separately. At armhole edge of each back on every row, dec 1 st 3 times. Work 14 rows even. Bind off. Pick up front sts. Dec 1 st at each edge of every row twice = 16 sts. Work 7 rows, bind off center 6 sts. Work each half separately. At each neck edge, dec 1 st twice. When the shoulders are the same length as back, bind off loosely.

SLEEVES: For the red dress. With smaller size needles and red, cast on 20 sts and work 4 rows in 1/1 ribbing. Change to larger size needles and work in dot pat, working 2 sts in each st across first row = 40 sts. Work 9 rows. At beg of next 2 rows, bind off 3 sts once, bind off 2 sts at beg of next 4 rows, bind off 3 sts at beg of next 4 rows. Bind off rem 14 sts.

POCKETS: With larger size needles and red or pink, cast on 12 sts and work 1 row in 1/1 ribbing, then work in dot pat for 10 rows. Knit first 2 sts tog at beg of next 4 rows. Bind off rem 8 sts. Make a 2nd pocket.

FINISHING: Sew shoulder seams. Sew sleeve seams. Gather sleeves and set in sleeves. With crochet hook and red or pink, work 1 round of sc along center back edge, and along lower edge of skirt work as foll: *1 sc, ch 3, 1 sc in the foll st, 1 sl st in the foll st*, rep * to *.

Fasten off. Sew on 2 snaps on back. With crochet hook and white, work 1 round of sc for the collar = 12 sc. On the next row, sl 1, 1 sc in the foll sc, 2 sc in the foll sc, 1 sc in each of the foll 6 sc, 2 sc in the foll sc, sl 1 in the last sc. Fasten off. Work same border along lower edge of skirt. With crochet hook and white, work 1 row of sc along edges of pockets. Fasten off. Sew on pockets. For the sleeveless dress, in pink, work 1 row of sc around armholes. Fasten off.

BLUE PANTS: Beg with lower edge of leg. With smaller size needles and blue, cast on 24 sts and work 4 rows in 1/1 ribbing. Change to larger size needles. Work 2 sts in each st across row = 48 sts. Work 2-3/4" (7 cm) in dot pat. Bind off 2 sts at beg of next 2 rows, bind off 1 st at beg of next 4 rows. Place sts on holder and make a 2nd leg. Place sts for both legs on the same needle and work 1-1/2" (4 cm). Change to smaller size needles and k2 tog across row = 40 sts. Work 4 rows and bind off loosely. With smaller size needles, pick up 5 sts at each edge of center 9 sts. Work 30 rows in 1/1 ribbing. Bind off center st. On foll row, cast on 1 st over bound off st. Work 2 rows even, then bind off loosely.

FINISHING: Sew side and inseams. Sew on buttons.

Clown Dolls

▼ Materials

Mayflower Cotton 8 (50 g) 1 ball each Yellow and Turquoise, or Pink and Blue, or Pink and Yellow; U.S. size 2 and 3 (2.5 and 3 mm) knitting needles

▼ Gauge

U.S. size 3 (3 mm) needles in St st: 4" (10 cm) = 26 sts x 36 rows.

To save time, take time to check gauge!

▼ Directions

PANTS: With smaller size needles and yellow, cast on 30 sts and work 3 rows in 1/1 ribbing.

Change to larger size needles, work in striped St st: *4 rows turquoise, 4 rows yellow*, rep * to *. Inc 1 st at each edge of every 4th row 3 times = 36 sts. Work 30 rows total. The last stripe is turquoise. Dec 1 st at right edge. Place 35 sts on holder. Work left piece in the same way, dec 1 st at left edge. With smaller size needles and yellow, join the 2 pieces, with dec edges at center = 70 sts. Dec 18 sts evenly spaced across first row = 52 sts. Work 6 rows in 1/1 ribbing. Bind off. Sew inseams and center front and back seams.

VEST: Worked from side to side. With smaller size needles and yellow, cast on 41 sts and work 3 rows in 1/1 ribbing.

Change to larger size needles, work in striped St st, alternating 2 rows in yellow and 2 rows of turquoise. After the 2nd row, divide into 3 pieces: Work 10 sts for left front, bind off 2 sts, work 17 sts for back, bind off 2 sts, work 10 sts for right front. Work first 10 sts for right front. At left edge, dec 1 st every 2nd row twice. Work 10 rows total on rem 8 sts, then shape neck. At right edge of every 2nd row, dec 1 st 4 times. Work rem 4 sts for a total of 20 rows above ribbing. The last stripe is

turquoise. Place sts on holder. Work left front to correspond rev shapings. Pick up 17 sts for the back. At each edge of every 2nd row, dec 1 st twice. Work rem 13 sts for 16 rows total above ribbing. The last stripe is turquoise. Work 1 row in St st in yellow. Place sts on holder.

FINISHING: With smaller size needles and yellow, pick up and knit 34 sts along armhole edge and work 2 rows in 1/1 ribbing. Bind off. Cut a strand about 10" (25 cm). Attach to armhole border and sew shoulders tog st by st with 4 sts. With smaller size needles and yellow, pick up and knit 53 sts along the front and back neck and work 2 rows in 1/1 ribbing. Bind off.

HAT: With smaller size needles and yellow, cast on 30 sts and work 6 rows in 1/1 ribbing. Change to larger size needles and work in striped St st alternating 2 rows yellow and 2 rows turquoise. Dec 1 st at each edge of every 4th row 6 times = 18 sts. Work to 28 rows above ribbing. The last stripe is turquoise. Break yarn and leave a strand 16" (40 cm) long. Thread through rem sts and gather tightly. Sew seam. Make a pompom in turquoise and sew to top of hat.

▼ Materials

Thick cotton yarn, 1 ball each Pink, Black, Dark Blue, White, Blue, Yellow, and Red; 4 white buttons

▼ Gauge

U.S. size 4 (3.5 mm) needles in garter st: 4" (10 cm) = 16 sts x 28 rows.

To save time, take time to check gauge!

▼ Directions

BOY

LEGS: With dark blue, cast on 18 sts and work in garter st: Knit 20 rows = 10 ridges as follows: 16 rows in blue, continue in black. On row 20, knit every 3rd and 4th st tog. Work 3 rows. On foll row knit every 2nd and 3rd st tog. Break yarn and thread through rem sts. Make a 2nd leg.

SLEEVES: With dark blue, cast on 16 sts and work in garter st: 10 rows in dark blue, 2 rows in white, 2 rows in dark blue, change to pink. On row 17, knit every 3rd and 4th st tog = 12 sts. Work 3 rows even. On foll row, knit the 2nd and the 3rd sts tog. Break yarn and thread through rem sts.

BODY: With blue, cast on 40 sts and work in garter st: 12 rows in blue, 28 rows in dark blue, 18 rows in pink, complete in yellow. At the same time, after 36 rows: k8, k2 tog twice, k16, k2 tog twice, k8. Foll row: K5, bind off 8

sts, k10, bind off 8 sts, k5. Foll row: k20. After 40 rows, work in St st: Change to pink; Rows 1 and 2: Work 20 sts. Row 3: Work 2 sts in each st. Row 4: Work 40 sts. Row 5: K10, inc 1 st by working in the strand between the sts, k10, inc 1, k10. Rows 6-8: Work 42 sts. Row 9: K11, inc 1, k20, inc 1, k11. Rows 10-14: Work 44 sts. Row 15: K10, k2 tog, k20, k2 tog, k10. Rows 16-18: Work 42 sts. Row 19: K10, k2 tog, k18, k2 tog, k10. Row 20: Work 40 sts. Row 21: Knit every 2nd and 3rd st tog. Rows 22-24: Work 27 sts. Row 25: K2 tog across, end with k1. Break yarn and thread through rem sts.

Sew back seam of body and head. Stuff. Sew shoulders tog. Sew the lower edge of body. Thread yarn through the neck through the first row of the head. Sew the back and lower seam of legs and arms. Stuff the legs and arms and sew to body.

HAT: With dark blue, cast on 40 sts and work 3 rows of 1/1 ribbing. Change to white and work 2 rows of St st. Row 3: *K2, inc 1 st by working in the strand between the sts*, rep * to *, end with k2. Work 2 rows. Row 6: Knit (= ridge on right side of work). Knit 2 rows. Row 9: *K2, k2 tog*, rep * to *, end with k3. Knit 3 rows. Row 13: *K1, k2 tog*, rep * to *. Knit 3 rows. Row 17: K2 tog across. Break yarn and thread through rem sts. Make a small red pompom and sew to top of hat.

FINISHING: Embroider the eyes in blue in duplicate st. Embroider mouth in pink foll the chart. Embroider nose in red in duplicate st. Cut strands of yellow for hair 4" (10 cm) long and sew to head.

GIRL

Work same as boy, but for body work 16 rows in blue, complete in black. For sleeves, work 2 rows in dark blue, 2 rows in white, 4 rows in dark blue*, work * to * twice, end with pink. For body, work 12 rows in blue, *4 rows in dark blue, 2 rows in white*, work * to * 4 times, 4 rows in dark blue, complete with 18 rows in pink and end with yellow.

FINISHING: Embroider eyes in blue in duplicate st. Embroider nose in pink foll chart, and red and mouth in stem st with red. Make body same as boy. For hair, cut strands of yellow 16" (40 cm) long for braids. For bangs, cut strands 4" (10 cm) long. Sew long strands to center of head, with a double row of sts along center of head. Make braids and tie ends with red yarn. Fold strands for bangs and sew to top of head. Sew 2 buttons to each shoulder.

CHART for Face

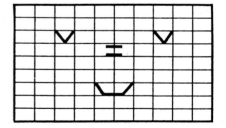

Just for Kids!

Teddy Bear Bag

▼ Materials

Mayflower Cotton 12 (50 g) 1 ball White; Mayflower Maxi (100 g) 1 ball Light Blue; Mayflower Cotton 8 (50 g) 1 ball each Dark Yellow, Turquoise, Brown, Dark Brown, White, Dark Pink, Red, Orange, Blue and Yellow; U.S. size 2 (2.5 mm) knitting needles; yellow vinyl 24" x 26" (60 x 65 cm), striped ribbon 2" (5 cm) wide to fit around top plus 3/4" (2 cm), 6 grommets 1/4" (1 cm) wide, 1-1/4 yd (1 m) thick cord, 2 buttons, cardboard

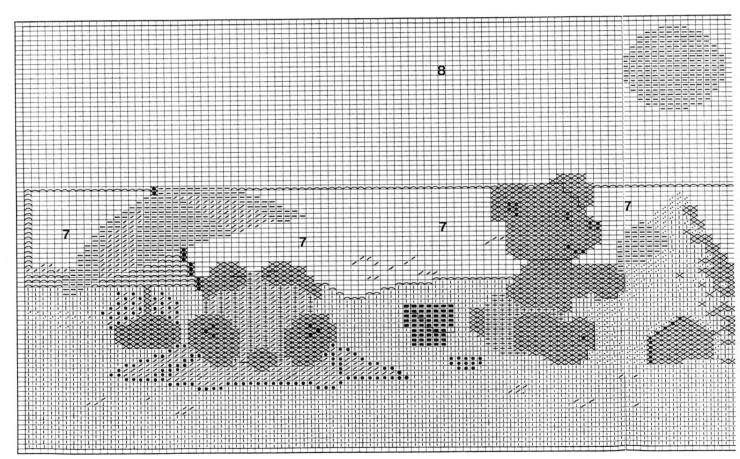

▼ Gauge

U.S. size 2 (2.5 mm) needles in St st: 4" (10 cm) = 26 sts x 36 rows.

To save time, take time to check gauge!

▼ Directions

NOTE: Embroider the motifs in duplicate stitch on finished work. For tweedy blue, knit with 1 strand of Cotton 10 and 1 strand of Maxi.

With dark yellow, cast on 162 sts and work in St st as foll: 36 rows of dark yellow, 18 rows of turquoise, continue in tweedy blue until piece measures 14-3/4" (37 cm). Bind off.

BOTTOM: With dark yellow, cast on 13 sts and work in St st. Cast on 4 sts at beg of every row twice. Cast on 3 sts at beg of every row 4 times. Inc 1 st at beg of every row 18 times. At each edge of every 4th row, inc 1 st twice = 55 sts. Work 12 rows without incs. At each edge of every 4th row, dec 1 st twice. At beg of every row, dec 1 st 18 times,

bind off 3 sts at beg of every row 4 times, bind off 4 sts at beg of every row twice. Bind off 13 sts.

FINISHING: Embroider motifs foll chart. Embroider black lines of chart in stem sts in dark brown around bears and in white on sand and water. Cut pieces of yellow vinyl the same size as the bottom of the bag and the bag with 1/4" (1 cm) seam allowance. Cut out a piece of cardboard the same size as bottom without seam allowance. Sew the bag together with a 1/4" (1 cm) seam and attach the bottom of the bag. Place the cardboard at the bottom of the bag, then insert plastic lining. Cut a piece of ribbon the same circumference as the top of the bag plus 3/4" (2 cm) seam allowance. Sew ends together. Make a 1/4" (1 cm) hem on both sides and sew top of bag to lower edge of band by placing right sides tog, then folding up to outside. Attach grommets evenly spaced around top band. Thread cord through grommets. Make knots at end of cord.

KEY TO CHART

X	= Brown
X	= Dark Brown
■	= Dark Pink
+	= Red
—	= Orange
●	= Blue
∴	= Yellow
/	= White
I	= Dark Yellow
⌣	and 7 = Turquoise

8= Tweedy Blue

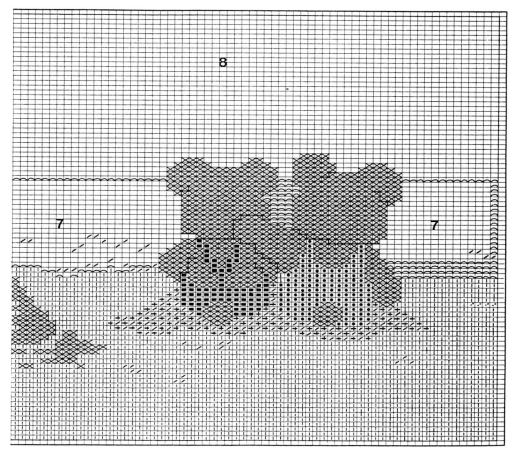

Sheriff Pullover

FINISHED MEASUREMENTS

Sizes 5 (6, 7) years

Chest 28-3/4" (29-1/2", 30-1/4") - 72 (74, 76) cm

Length 17-1/4" (18", 18-3/4") - 43 (45, 47) cm

Sleeve Length 12" (12-3/4", 13-1/4") - 30.5 (32, 33.5) cm

▼ Materials

Mayflower Cotton 8 (50 g) 2 (3, 3) balls White, 1 ball each Black, Gray, Red, Moss Green, Gold, Orange-Gold, Blue, Dark Brown, Medium Brown and Light Brown; U.S. size 2 and 3 (2.5 and 3 mm) knitting needles, 16" circular needle U.S. size 2 (2.5 mm)

▼ Gauge

U.S. size 3 (3 mm) needles in St st: 4" (10 cm) = 26 sts x 36 rows.

To save time, take time to check gauge!

▼ Directions

BACK: With smaller size needles and green, cast on 80 (82, 84) sts and work 2" (5 cm) in 1/1 ribbing. Purl 1 row on wrong side of work, inc 15 (16, 17) sts evenly spaced across row = 95 (98, 101) sts.

Change to larger size needles, work in striped St st as foll: 6 (10, 14) rows in dark brown, 88 rows in white, 2 rows in black, complete in gray.

When piece measures 17-1/4" (18", 18-3/4") - 42 (45, 47) cm from beg, bind off 28 (29, 30) sts, place center 39 (40, 41) sts on holder, bind off 28 (29, 30) sts. FRONT: Beg front same as back, but work by foll chart, beg with 1 border st and point 1 (2, 3), work to point 4 (5, 6), end with 1 border st. Beg with row indicated by A (B, C). When piece measures 15" (16", 16-3/4") - 38 (40, 42) cm = point D (E, F) on the chart. Bind off center 17 (18, 19) sts. Join 2nd ball of yarn to 2nd part and work at the same time. At each neck edge of every 2nd row, bind off 3 sts once, bind off 2 sts twice, dec 1 st 4 times. Work rem 28

(29, 30) sts on each shoulder until piece measures 17-1/4" (18", 18-3/4") - 43 (45, 47) cm = point G (H, I) on chart. Bind off.

SLEEVE: With smaller size needles and black, cast on 48 (50, 52) sts, work 1-1/2" (4 cm) in 1/1 ribbing. Purl 1 row on wrong side of work, inc 13 (14, 15) sts evenly spaced across row = 61 (64, 67) sts. Change to larger size needles, work in striped St st as foll: 9 (10, 11) rows in gray, 2 rows in black, 17 (18, 19) rows in green, 2 rows in black, 14 (15, 16) rows in white, 4 rows in black, 20 (21, 22) rows in white, 4 rows in black, complete in red. At the same time, inc 1 st at each edge of every 8th row 0 (0, 2) times. Inc 1 st at each edge of every 6th row 12 (15, 14) times. Inc 1 st at each edge of every 4th row 4 (1, 0) times. Work new sts in St st as you inc = 93 (96, 99) sts.

When sleeve measures 12" (12-3/4", 13-1/4") - 30.5 (32, 33.5) cm from beg, bind off all sts.

FINISHING: Embroider front in duplicate st. Sew shoulder seams. With circular needle and red, pick up and knit 100 (104, 108) sts around neck. Work 1-1/4" (3.5 cm) in 1/1 ribbing, bind off.

Sew sleeves to side seams, matching center of sleeve to shoulder seams. Sew side and sleeve seams.

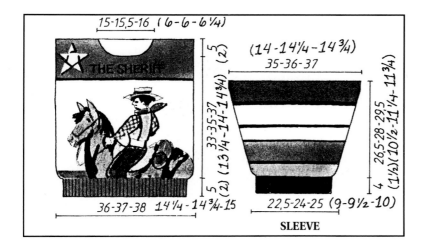

Charts for Sheriff Pullover continued on next page.

KEY TO CHART

	Color	Color #		Color	Color #		Color	Color #		Color	Color #
I or 1	= White	502	=	= Red	510	/	= Orange-gold	509	–	= Med. Brown	593
●	= Black	515	+	= Moss Green	560	×	= Blue	506	\	= Light Brown	536
V or 2	= Gray	581	H	= Gold	551	X	= Dark Brown	555			

Holiday Sweater, Hat, Booties, and Mittens

▼ Materials

Neveda Skol (50 g) 2 (3, 3) balls White and 1 ball Red for pullover, 1 ball White and small amount of Red for hat, 1 ball White and small amount of Red for socks, 1 ball White and small amount of Red for mittens; U.S. size 2 and 3 (2.5 and 3 mm) knitting needles; 6 buttons

▼ Gauge

U.S. size 3 (3 mm) needles in St st: 4" (10 cm) = 26 sts x 34 rows.

To save time, take time to check gauge!

▼ Directions

SWEATER

BACK: With smaller size needles and red, cast on 58 (60, 62) sts, purl 1 row with white and work 1-1/4" (3 cm) in 1/1 ribbing. Purl 1 row on wrong side, inc 6 (7, 8) sts evenly spaced across row = 64 (67, 70) sts.

Change to larger size needles, work in St st as foll: 2 rows in white, 5 rows foll chart 1, beg with 1 border st, work from point 1 (2, 3) to point 4 once, then point 4 to 5, 3 (3, 4) times, then point 5 (4, 5) to point 6 (5, 7) once, 1 border st. Carry unused yarn loosely across wrong side of work. Continue in white until piece measures 10-1/4" (10-3/4", 11-1/4") - 26 (27, 28.5) cm. Bind off center 26 (27, 28) sts. Join 2nd ball of yarn to 2nd part and work at the same time. Work 19 (20, 21) sts for 3/4" (2 cm) in 1/1 ribbing. Bind off sts

on each shoulder.

FRONT: Work front same as back.

Shape Neck: When piece measures 9" (9-1/4", 10") - 22.5 (23.5, 25) cm from beg, bind off center 20 (21, 22) sts. Join 2nd ball of yarn to 2nd part and work at the same time. At each neck edge of every row, bind off 2 sts once, dec 1 st once. Work until piece measures 9-1/2" (10", 10-1/2") - 24 (25, 26.5) cm, continue in 1/1 ribbing. After 1/4" (1 cm), make 2 buttonholes on each shoulder. From side seam, work 6 (6, 7) sts, bind off 2 sts, work 5 (6, 6) sts, bind off 2 sts, work to end of row. On foll row, cast on 2 sts over bound off sts. When piece measures 10-1/4" (10-3/4", 11-1/4") - 26 (27, 28.5) cm, bind off all sts.

CHART 1

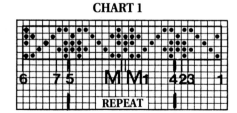

REPEAT

CHART 2

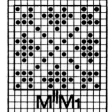

KEY TO CHARTS

- ● = Red
- ☐ = White

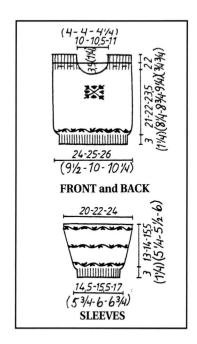

FRONT and BACK

SLEEVES

SLEEVE: With smaller size needles and red, cast on 32 (34, 36) sts. Purl 1 row in white. Work 1-1/4" (3 cm) in 1/1 ribbing. Purl 1 row on wrong side of work, inc 8 (9, 10) sts evenly spaced across row = 40 (43, 46) sts.

Change to larger size needles, work in striped St st: 2 rows white, *5 rows foll chart 1, center chart at point M (M1, M), 12 (14, 16) rows in white*, rep * to * end with 5 rows of chart, complete in white. At the same time, inc 1 st each edge of every 4th row 3 (3, 4) times. Inc 1 st each edge of every 6th row 5 times. Work new sts in St st and pattern as you inc = 54 (59, 64) sts.

When sleeve measures 6-1/2" (6-3/4", 7-1/4") - 16 (17, 18.5) cm from beg, bind off all sts.

FINISHING: Embroider motif on front foll chart 2, centering chart at point M

(M1, M), beg 4-1/2" (4-3/4", 4-3/4") - 11.5 (12, 12.5) cm above ribbing. With smaller size needles and white, pick up and knit 37 (39, 41) sts around back neck and work 3/4" (2 cm) in 1/1 ribbing, bind off in red. With smaller size needles and white, pick up and knit 41 (43, 45) sts around front neck and work 3/4" (2 cm) in 1/1 ribbing, bind off in red. Make 1 buttonhole 3 sts from each edge when border measures 1/4" (1 cm). For each buttonhole, bind off 2 sts. On foll row, cast on 2 sts over bound off sts. Sew on buttons and button shoulder borders, tack ends in place. Sew sleeves to side seams. Sew side and sleeve seams.

HAT
With smaller size needles and red, cast on 98 (114) sts, change to white and purl 1 row, then work 2-1/2" (6 cm) in 1/1 ribbing.

Change to larger size needles and work in St st. Work 2 rows in white, 15 rows

in chart 1, beg and end with 1 border st and working rep 6 times. After the 15th row, continue in white until piece measures 5-1/2" (6-1/4") - 14 (16) cm from beg, end wrong side of work. Work next row as foll: 1 border st, k1, sl 1, k1, psso, k10, *k2 tog, k2, sl 1, k1, psso, k10*, rep * to * 5 (6) times, k2 tog, k1, 1 border st. Work these dec every 4th row 3 times and every 2nd row twice. Work dec above previous ones. When 26 (30) sts rem, piece will measure 7-1/2" (8-1/4") - 19 (21) cm. K2 tog across. Break yarn and thread through rem sts.

FINISHING: Embroider last 11 rows of chart 1 (bird motif) in duplicate st. Sew back seam. Tack down small pleats at top of hat as shown in photo. Fold border in half to outside. Make a pompom 1-1/2" (4 cm) in diameter in white and red (twice as much red as white). Sew pompom to top of hat.

SOCKS
With larger size needles and red, cast on 30 sts. Change to white and purl 1 row, then work in 1/1 ribbing for 1-1/4" (3.5 cm). Change to smaller size needles and work 2-3/4" (7 cm) in 1/1 ribbing ending on right side of work. Change to larger size needles and continue in St st, knitting the first row, then work 2 (4, 6) rows in St st. Place last 15 sts on holder and work in short rows over first 15 sts for heel. Row 1: K15, turn, sl the first st, work 14 sts, turn. Row 3: Sl the first st, work 13 sts, turn. Continue in this way working 1 st less until 7 sts rem. Now work 1 additional st at end of next 8 rows = 15 sts. Pick up 15 sts from holder = 30 sts and work in St st for 1-1/2" (2", 2-1/2") - 4 (5, 6) cm, ending on wrong side of work. Work the toe as foll: k2, sl 1, k1,

psso, k8, k2 tog, k2, sl 1, k1, psso, k8, k2 tog, k2. Rep these dec on every 2nd row 3 times, maintaining 2 sts between dec = 14 sts. Knit the first 7 sts tog with the last 7 sts. Embroider the motif in red by foll chart 2 on toe. Fold ribbing to outside. Make a 2nd sock, working heel over last 15 sts.

RED SOCKS

With smaller size needles and white, cast on 30 sts. Change to red and work 1" (2.5 cm) in 1/1 ribbing, end on wrong side of work. Change to larger size needles and work in St st. Work 2 rows in red, 5 rows foll chart 3 as foll: 1 border st, work from point 1 to 2, 1 border st. Work 4 (6, 8) rows in red. Work heel and toe as on white socks. Make a 2nd sock, working heel over last 15 sts.

MITTENS

With larger size needles and red, cast on 34 sts. Change to white and purl 1 row, then continue in 1/1 ribbing for 1-1/4" (3 cm). Continue in St st for 2-1/2" (2-3/4", 3") - 6.5 (7, 7.5) cm, ending on wrong side of work. Foll row: K2, sl 1, k1, psso, k10, k2 tog, k2, sl 1, k1 psso, k10, k2 tog, k2. Rep these dec on every 2nd row 3 times until there are 2 sts between the dec = 18 sts. Knit the first 9 sts tog with the last 9 sts to close end. Embroider the motif in red foll last 9 rows of chart 1 in duplicate st. Beg on the 4th (5th, 6th) row above border and the 5th st from the right edge. Rev the same motif on the 2nd mitten. Beg 22 sts from the right edge. Sew seam. Make a red cord 32" (80 cm) long and sew to inside edge of both mittens.

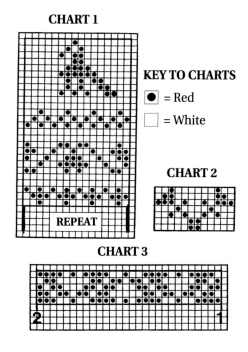

CHART 1

KEY TO CHARTS

● = Red

☐ = White

REPEAT

CHART 2

CHART 3

2   1

Animal Mittens

<table>
<tr><td colspan="2">

FINISHED MEASUREMENTS

Sizes
1 (2) years
Width
6" (6-3/4") - 15 (17) cm
Length
4-1/2" (5") - 11.5 (12.5) cm

</td></tr>
</table>

▼ Materials

Neveda Skol (50 g) 1 ball Red or Blue, 1 ball Gray or White Angora; U.S. size 3 and 4 (3 and 3.5 mm) knitting needles

▼ Gauge

U.S. size 4 (3.5 mm) needles in St st: 4" (10 cm) = 21 sts x 29 rows.

To save time, take time to check gauge!

▼ Directions

BACK: With smaller size needles and red or blue, cast on 34 (36) sts and work 1-1/2" (4 cm) in 1/1 ribbing.

103

CHART 1

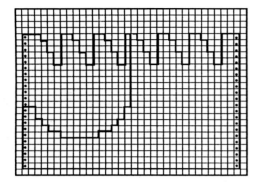

CHART 2

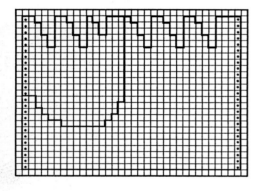

KEY TO CHARTS

● = 1 border st

☐ = St st

Change to larger size needles, work in jacquard St st by foll chart 1 (2). Be sure to cross yarns when changing from Angora to Skol and vice versa. On the 17th (20th) row, dec 1 st 6 times. Rep these dec on the 20th (23rd) and the 22nd (25th) rows. Break yarn and thread through rem 16 (18) sts. Make a 2nd mitten by rev chart. (Beg first row at left edge.)

THUMB: With larger size needles and red or blue, cast on 2 sts and work in St st. Inc 1 st at each edge of every row 4 (5) times = 10 (12) sts and 5 (6) rows. On the foll 4 (5) rows, work k1, k2 tog, work to last 3 sts, k2 tog, k1. Break yarn through rem sts and sew seam.

EARS: With larger size needles and gray or white, cast on 12 sts and work in St st. At each edge of every row, dec 1 st 6 times. Fold the ear in half and sew edges. Sew slanted edge to top of head.

SNOUT: With larger size needles and gray or white, cast on 6 sts and work in St st. Inc at each edge of first and 2nd row = 10 sts and 4 rows. Dec 1 st at each edge of foll 2 rows. Bind off rem 6 sts.

FINISHING: Thread yarn around ends of snout and stuff. Sew to head. Embroider the eyes, nose and whiskers in black. Sew thumb to side one row above ribbing. Sew side seams.

Polar Bear Sweater, Hat, and Mittens

▼ Materials

Neveda Skol (50 g) 1 (2, 2) balls Royal, 1 ball each Light Blue, Dark Blue, Light Yellow, Baby Blue, Gray, and Blue Gray, 25 (30, 35) g of White Angora; U.S. size 3 and 5 (3 and 3.75 mm) knitting needles, 16" circular needle U.S. size 3 (3 mm)

▼ Gauge

U.S. size 5 (3.75 mm) needles in St st: 4" (10 cm) = 21 sts x 27 rows.

To save time, take time to check gauge!

▼ Directions

SWEATER

BACK: With smaller size needles and dark blue, cast on 62 (66, 72) sts and

KEY TO CHARTS

- ⊡ = Light Yellow
- ☒ = White
- 工 = Blue Gray
- ⊙ = Gray
- ◣ = Baby Blue
- ◢ = Light Blue
- ▬ = Dark Blue
- ☐ = Royal

CHART 1

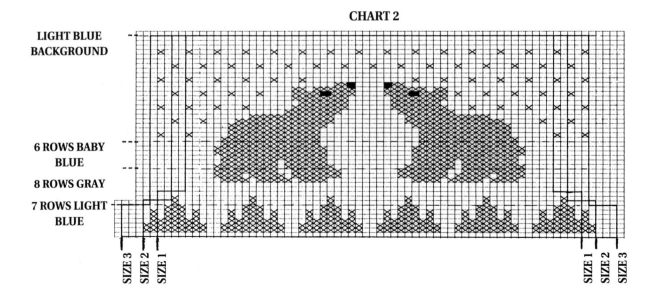

REPEAT

work in striped 1/1 ribbing as foll: 2 rows dark blue, 2 rows royal, 2 rows light blue, 2 rows baby blue, 2 rows light yellow, 2 rows gray, 2 rows blue gray = 14 rows.

Change to larger size needles, work in fairisle St st by foll chart 1. Beg at point C (B, A) and work to point D = 22 (31, 40) rows, then foll chart 2 (glaciers, bears and snowflakes will be embroidered in duplicate st later). Carry yarn loosely across back of work. Shape armholes as shown on chart. Bind off 4 sts at beg of next 2 rows = 54 (58, 64) sts. When armhole measures 4-1/2" (5", 5-1/4") - 11.5 (12.5, 13.5) cm, change to smaller size needles and yellow and work in 1/1 ribbing, inc 1 st on first row. On the 5th row, bind off the center 19 (21, 23) sts. Join 2nd ball of yarn to 2nd half and work at the same time. Work 5 rows in 1/1 ribbing, bind off 18 (19, 21) sts on each shoulder.

FRONT: Beg front same as back. After the 14th row of light blue of chart 2, bind off center 8 (10, 12) sts. Join 2nd ball of yarn to 2nd half and work at the same time. At each neck edge of every 2nd row, bind off 3 sts once, bind off 2 sts once. When chart is complete, place sts on holder. With smaller size needles and blue gray, pick up 18 (19, 21) sts from shoulder, pick up 21 (23, 25) sts along neck edge and 18 (19, 21) sts from 2nd shoulder. In 1/1 ribbing, work 1 row of blue gray, 2 rows of gray and 2 rows of yellow. Bind off loosely.

SLEEVE: With smaller size needles and dark blue, cast on 32 (34, 36) sts, work in striped 1/1 ribbing as on back, inc 11 (12, 11) sts evenly spaced across last row = 43 (46, 47) sts.

Change to larger size needles, work in jacquard St st foll chart 1. For size 1 year, work from point E to D. For size 2

CHART 2

LIGHT BLUE BACKGROUND

6 ROWS BABY BLUE

8 ROWS GRAY

7 ROWS LIGHT BLUE

SIZE 3 SIZE 2 SIZE 1   SIZE 1 SIZE 2 SIZE 3

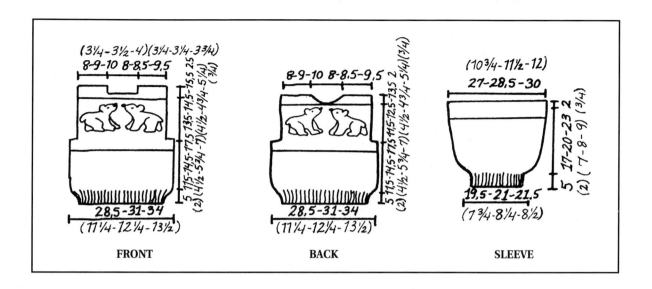

FRONT **BACK** **SLEEVE**

yrs, work from point F to H and E to D. For size 3 years, work from point G to H and E to D, end with 6 rows of light blue and 7 rows of gray. At the same time, inc 1 st each edge of every 5th (6th, 6th) row 8 (8, 9) times. Work new sts in St st and pat st as you inc = 59 (62, 65) sts.

When sleeve measures 9-3/4" (10", 11") - 22 (25, 28) cm from beg, bind off all sts.

FINISHING: Embroider glaciers, bears and snowflakes in duplicate st with angora foll chart. Beg the glaciers on the 2nd row of light blue. Make 4 glaciers on the first 2 sizes and 6 glaciers on the largest size. Embroider 5 glaciers on the sleeves so that the center one is over the center 9 sts. Embroider the eyes and nose of the bears in dark blue in satin stitch. Outline the bears in gray blue in stem stitch. Overlap the front border over the back. Attach snaps on shoulders. See photo.

HAT
With smaller size needles and dark blue, cast on 82 (90, 98) sts and work 14 rows of striped ribbing as on the back of sweater. Change to larger size needles and blue gray and work in St st for 7" (8", 8-3/4") - 18 (20, 22) cm and work the last 5 rows of jacquard chart 1. Work 6 rows of blue gray in St st. On the 3rd row, dec 20 (22, 24) sts by knitting every 3rd and 4th sts tog = 62 (68, 74) sts, then work 13 rows of baby blue, dec on the first (5th, 7th, 9th, 11th) row as in the 3rd row of blue gray by knitting the 3rd and 4th sts tog. After the 12th row you will have 17 (19, 20) sts. Row 13: 1 border st, k1 (1, 0), k2 tog 7 (8, 9) times, 1 border st. Break yarn and thread through rem sts. Sew seam. Make a pompom 2-3/4" (7 cm) in diameter in blue and gray and sew to top of hat.

MITTENS
With smaller size needles and dark blue, cast on 24 (26, 28) sts and work 1-1/2" (4 cm) in 1/1 ribbing. Change to larger size needles and gray and work in St st. Work 4 rows of gray, 8 (14, 18) rows of light blue, 8 rows of royal. Over the last 8 rows, dec in the 3rd, 5th, 7th row by knitting every 3rd and 4th st tog. Break yarn and thread through rem 12 (13, 14) sts. Thumb: With larger size needles and yellow, cast on 2 sts. At each edge of every row, inc 1 st 4 (5, 6) times = 10 (12, 14) sts. Work 5 (7, 9) sts even. On foll row, k1, k2 tog, work to last 3 sts, k2 tog, k1. Break yarn and thread through rem sts. Embroider snowflakes in duplicate st on the light blue stripe. Sew the slanted edge of the thumb to the mitten, beg 1 row above the ribbing. Sew the seam. Make a 2nd mitten. Make a cord of dark blue 36" (90 cm) long. Sew to ribbing edge of both mittens.

Legwarmers

FINISHED MEASUREMENTS

10" x 36" (25 x 91 cm)

▼ Materials

Scheepjeswol Invicta Extra (50 g) 3 balls Turquoise, tapestry wool in indicated colors; U.S. size 2 and 3 (2.5 and 3 mm) knitting needles

▼ Gauge

U.S. size 3 (3 mm) needles in St st: 4" (10 cm) = 28 sts x 38 rows.

To save time, take time to check gauge!

▼ Directions

BACK: With smaller size needles and turquoise, cast on 72 sts and work 1-1/2" (4 cm) in 1/1 ribbing.

Change to larger size needles and work in St st for 12-3/4" (32 cm) from beg. Change to smaller size needles and work 1-1/2" (4 cm) in 1/1 ribbing. Bind off. Make 2nd legwarmer.

FINISHING: Embroider motifs in duplicate st foll chart, beg 6-1/4" (16 cm) from lower edge and centering chart. Sew center back seam.

KEY TO CHART

·	= Ecru	◥	= Light Yellow
I	= Salmon	✕	= Yellow
—	= Light Pink	✕	= Dark Green
╱	= Rose	▬	= Hunter Green
▐	= Pumpkin	✕	= Blue
●	= Red	◣	= Black
○	= Wine		

109

Goldfish Sweater

▼ Materials

Mayflower Cotton 8 (50 g) 2 balls Orange, 1 ball each Turquoise, Light Yellow, Pink, Pumpkin and Black; U.S. size 2 and 4 (2.5 and 3.5 mm) knitting needles; 4 buttons

▼ Gauge

U.S. size 4 (3.5 mm) needles in St st: 4" (10 cm) = 24 sts x 35 rows.

To save time, take time to check gauge!

▼ Directions

BACK: With smaller size needles and orange, cast on 70 (76) sts and work 1" (2.5 cm) in 1/1 ribbing.

Change to larger size needles, work in St st.

Shape Armholes: When back measures 6-3/4" (8") - 17 (20) cm from beg, bind off 4 sts at beg of next 2 rows. Dec 1 st at each edge of every 2nd row 3 times = 56 (62) sts. When armhole measures 1-3/4" (4.5 cm), shape neck. Bind off center 10 sts. Join 2nd ball of yarn to 2nd part and work at the same time. Cast on 1 st at each edge and work rem 24 (27) sts at each side.

When armhole measures 4-3/4" (5-1/4") - 12 (13 cm) from beg, bind off rem 12 (14) sts on each shoulder.

FRONT: Beg front same as back.

When armhole measures 2-1/2" (6.5 cm) from beg, bind off center 14 (16) sts. Join 2nd ball of yarn to 2nd part and work at the same time. At each neck

edge of every 2nd row, bind off 2 sts twice, dec 1 st 5 times. Work rem 12 (14) sts until piece measures 4-3/4" (5-1/4") - 12 (13 cm) from beg. Bind off all sts.

SLEEVE: With smaller size needles and orange, cast on 30 (32) sts, work 3/4" (2 cm) in 1/1 ribbing. Purl 1 row on wrong side of work row, inc 30 (32) by working 2 sts in each st = 60 (64) sts.

Change to larger size needles and turquoise and work in St st. When piece measures 2-1/4" (2-1/2") - 5.5 (6.5) cm from beg, shape cap.

Bind off 7 sts at beg of next 2 rows. Bind off 2 sts at beg of next 12 (14) rows. Bind off 4 sts at beg of next 2 rows. Bind off rem 14 sts.

POCKET: With larger size needles and turquoise, cast on 19 sts and work in St st by foll chart, omitting fish. Inc and dec by foll chart. Work last 6 rows in light yellow in 1/1 ribbing. Bind off. Embroider the fish and bubbles in duplicate stitch.

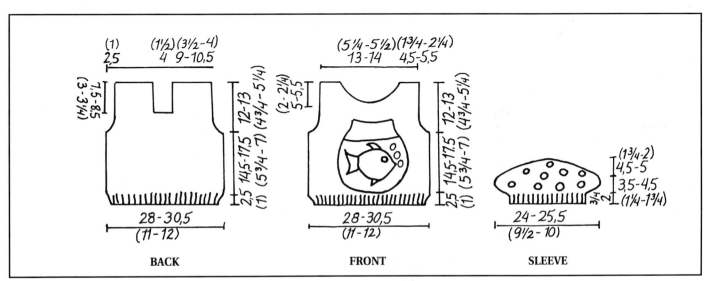

| BACK | FRONT | SLEEVE |

FINISHING: Embroider large and small dots on sleeves, using the photo as a guide. Sew on pocket to the front. Place the lower edge of the pocket 8 rows above the border.

Sew shoulder seams.

NECKBAND: With smaller size needles and orange, pick up and knit 69 (77) sts around neck and work 3/4" (2 cm)

in 1/1 ribbing, bind off. With smaller size needles and orange, pick up and knit 24 (28) sts from left back opening edge and work 3/4" (2 cm). Bind off. Work same border on right back. Sew border ends in place and make 4 buttonclasps on right edge. Sew on buttons. Set in sleeves and sew side and sleeve seams.

KEY TO CHART

1	= turquoise	◣	= pink
·	= light yellow	◪	= pumpkin
X	= orange	V	= black

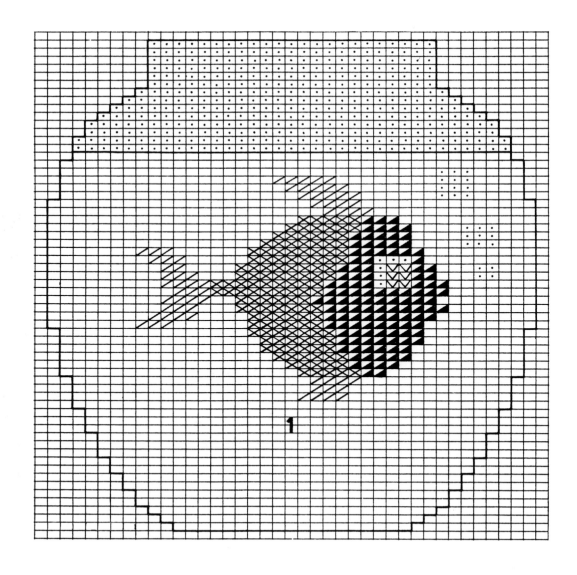

Mouse Pullover and Mittens

▼ Materials

PULLOVER
Scheepjeswol Invicta Extra (50 g) 1 (2) balls each Ocher and Red, 1 ball each Blue and White, Tapestry wool in indicated colors; U.S. size 2 and 3 (2.5 and 3 mm) knitting needles

MITTENS
Scheepjeswol Superwash Zermatt 1 ball each Blue, Green and Red; 3 buttons; U.S. size 5 (3.75 mm) knitting needles

▼ Gauge

U.S. size 3 (3 mm) needles in St st with Invicta Extra: 4" (10 cm) = 28 sts x 34 rows.

U.S. size 5 (4.5 mm) needles in St st with Superwash Zermatt: 4" (10 cm) = 20 sts.

To save time, take time to check gauge!

▼ Directions

PULLOVER
BACK: With smaller size needles and ocher, cast on 86 (90) sts and work 1-1/4" (3 cm) in 1/1 ribbing.

Change to larger size needles and red, work in fairisle St st by foll chart 2.

113

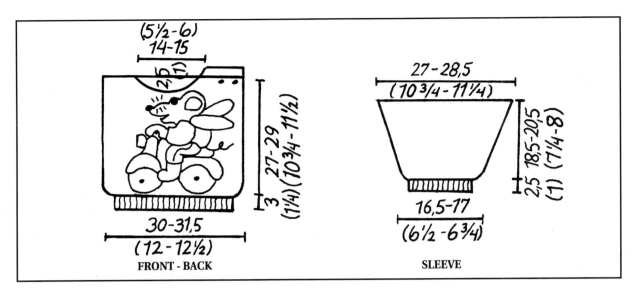

(5½-6)
14-15

26 (11)

27-29
(10¾-11½)

3 (1¼)

30-31,5
(12-12½)

FRONT - BACK

27 - 28,5
(10¾ - 11¼)

18,5-20,5
(7¼-8)

2,5 (1)

16,5-77
(6½ - 6¾)

SLEEVE

Work the dots in ocher. Carry unused yarn loosely across wrong side of work. When piece measures 11" (11-3/4") - 27.5 (29.5) cm from beg, bind off 23 (24) sts for the shoulder, place 40 (42) sts on a holder for neck and knit last 23 (24) sts with blue. Work 7 rows of 1/1 ribbing. Bind off loosely.

FRONT: Beg front same as back.

Change to larger size needles, work in striped St st as foll: 6 (8) rows in red, 2 (4) rows in blue and continue in ocher until piece measures 10" (10-3/4") - 25 (27) cm from beg. Place the center 18 (20) sts on a holder and work left half first. At neck edge of every 2nd row, bind off 3 sts 3 times, bind off 2 sts once. When piece measures 11" (11-3/4") - 27.5 (29.5) cm from beg, bind off 23 (24) sts for the shoulder. Pick up sts from right half. Work 4 rows in ocher, then 1 row in blue. Change to 1/1 ribbing and work until piece measures 12" (12-3/4") - 30 (32) cm from beg, making 2 buttonholes on 2nd row of 1/1 ribbing. 5 (6) sts from armhole edge, bind off 2 sts, work 8 sts, bind off 2 sts, work to end of row.

On foll row, cast on 2 sts over bound off sts. Bind off.

SLEEVE: With smaller size needles and red, cast on 48 (50) sts, work 1" (2.5 cm) in 1/1 ribbing.

Change to larger size needles, work in striped St st: *6 rows blue, 6 rows white*, rep * to *. At the same time, inc 1 st each edge of every 4th row 15 (16) times. Work new sts in St st as you inc = 78 (82) sts.

When sleeve measures 8-1/4" (9") - 21 (23) cm from beg, bind off all sts.

FINISHING: Embroider mouse motif in duplicate st by centering chart above blue stripe on front. Embroider the nose and whiskers in black in stem stitch. Sew right shoulder seam. With smaller size needles and blue, pick up and knit 95 (99) sts around neck and work in 1/1 ribbing. When neckband measures 1/2" and 1-1/4" (1.5 and 3.5 cm) from beg, make a buttonhole: right side facing, work 3 sts, bind off 2 sts, work to end of row. On foll row, cast on 2 sts over bound off sts. When neckband measures 2" (5 cm), bind off.

Fold neckband in half to inside and slip stitch in place, overlap front over back and tack in place. Sew on buttons and reinforce buttonholes. Sew sleeves to side seams, matching center of sleeve with shoulder seams. Sew side and sleeve seams.

MITTENS

With blue, cast on 30 sts and work 2-3/4" (7 cm) in 1/1 ribbing. Continue in St st, alternating 2 rows green and 2 rows red until piece measures 4-1/2" (11 cm) from beg. Work 2 rows in blue, dec 6 sts on the first row. Work 2 rows in green, dec 6 sts on the first row. Work 2 rows with red, dec 6 sts on the first row. Break yarn and thread through rem 12 sts and fasten off.

THUMB: With blue, cast on 2 sts and work in St st. Inc 1 st at beg of next 10 rows. Work 3/4" (2 cm) on these 12 sts. On foll row, k2 tog across. Break yarn and thread through 6 sts. Fasten off. Sew on thumb beg just above ribbing. Fold ribbing in half to outside. Make a 2nd mitten. Make a cord and sew to ribbing of each mitten.

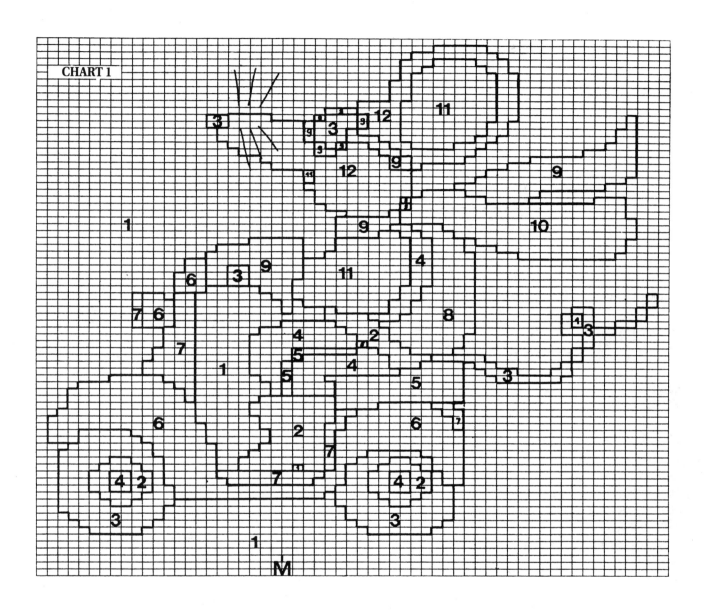

CHART 1

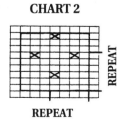

CHART 2

REPEAT

REPEAT

KEY TO CHARTS

1 and X = Ocher	7 = Dark Green
2 = Red	8 = Light Pink
3 = Black	9 = Pink
4 = Blue	10 = Light Yellow
5 = Dark Blue	11 = White
6 = Green	12 = Gray

▼ Materials

Mayflower Cotton 8 (50 g) 1 (1, 2) balls Red; U.S. size 2 and 3 (2.5 and 3 mm) knitting needles, U.S. size B/1 (2 mm) crochet hook; elastic thread

▼ Gauge

U.S. size 3 (3 mm) needles in St st: 4" (10 cm) = 26 sts x 34 rows.

To save time, take time to check gauge!

▼ Directions

WAIST BOTTOM: Worked in 1 piece, beg at waist of front. With smaller size needles, cast on 50 (53, 56) sts and work 4 rows in St st (first row is wrong side of work). Knit 1 row on wrong side and work 4 rows of St st. Change to larger size needles and work in St st. At each edge of every 2nd row, bind off 4 sts once, bind off 3 sts twice, bind off 2 sts twice, dec 1 st 6 times. At each edge of every 4th row, dec 1 st 1 (2, 3) times. Work 6 (8, 10) rows of St st over rem 8 (9, 10) sts. At each edge of every 2nd row, cast on 3 sts twice, inc 1 st 15 (16, 17) times = 50 (53, 56) sts. Change to smaller size needles, work 4 rows of St st, purl 1 row on right side of work, work 4 rows of St st. Bind off. With smaller size needles, pick up 59 (67, 75) sts along each leg opening and work 4 rows of 1/1 ribbing, knit 1 row on wrong side of work, work 4 rows of St st and bind off loosely. Fold casing in half to inside and slip stitch in place. Thread elastic through casing. Pick up 7 sts from each side and work 3/4" (2 cm) in garter st and place sts on holder. Make 2 cords 24" (60 cm) long. Thread each cord through sts and make a knot at each end.

TOP: Made of 2 triangles. With smaller size needles, cast on 29 (31, 33) sts, work 4 rows of St st, purling the first row for wrong side of work. Knit 1 row on wrong side, then work 4 rows of St st. Change to larger size needles, working 3 sts at each edge in garter st. Slip the first st. On right side of work rows, work as foll: Sl 1, k1, k2 tog in back of sts, knit to last 4 sts, k2 tog, k1, k1 in back of st. Work decreases 11 (12, 13) times total = 7 sts on needle. Following row (right side of work): Sl 1, k1, k3 tog, k1, k1 in back of st. Next row:

Sl 1, k3, k1 in back of st. Next row: Sl 1, k3 tog, k1 in back of st. Work rem 3 sts for 4 rows, then place sts on holder.

FINISHING: Block pieces. Fold the underside of each piece at ridge line to inside and sew in place. Make a cord 30" (75 cm) long and 2 cords 22" (55 cm) long. Thread the long cord through the lower borders of the top. Thread 1 cord through 3 sts on holder at top of each triangle and fasten in place. Make a knot at each end. See photo.

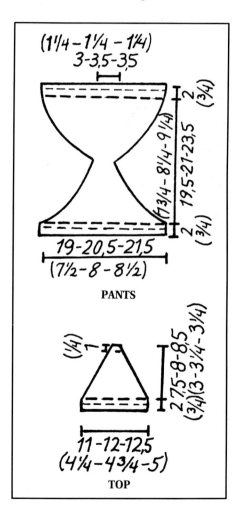

Snowflake Pullover

▼ Materials

Scheepjeswol Superwash Zermatt (50 g): 4 (5, 6) balls White, 2 balls Blue, 1 ball Light Blue; U.S. size 4 and 6 (3.5 and 4 mm) knitting needles, 16" circular needle U.S. size 4 (3.5 mm)

▼ Gauge

U.S. size 4 (3.5 mm) needles in St st: 4" (10 cm) = 18 sts x 24 rows.

To save time, take time to check gauge!

▼ Directions

BACK: With smaller size needles and blue, cast on 52 (56, 58) sts and work 1-1/2" (4 cm) in striped 1/1 ribbing: 1 row in blue on right side of work, *2 rows in white, 2 rows in blue*, rep * to *. Purl 1 row on wrong side of work, inc 13 (13, 15) sts evenly spaced across last row = 65 (69, 73) sts.

Change to larger size needles, work in St st.

When piece measures 16-1/2" (18-1/2", 20-1/2") - 41.5 (46.5, 51.5) cm from beg, bind off center 21 (23, 25) sts. Join 2nd ball of yarn to 2nd part and work at the same time. At each neck edge of every 2nd row, bind off 2 sts once. Dec 1 st 0 (1, 1) time. When piece measures 17" (19", 21") - 43 (48, 53) cm, bind off rem 20 (20, 21) sts.

FRONT: Beg front same as back. When piece measures 15" (17-1/4", 18-3/4") - 38 (43, 47) cm from beg, bind off center 13 (15, 17) sts. Join 2nd ball of yarn to 2nd part and work at the same time. At each neck edge of every 2nd row, bind off 2 sts twice, dec 1 st twice. Work rem 20 (20, 21) sts on each shoulder until piece measures 17" (18",18-3/4") - 43 (45, 47) cm. Bind off.

SLEEVE: With smaller size needles and white, cast on 34 (36, 36) sts, work 1-1/2" (4 cm) in striped 1/1 ribbing as on back. Purl 1 row on wrong side of work, inc 9 (9, 10) sts evenly spaced across row = 43 (45, 46) sts.

Change to larger size needles and white, work in St st. Inc 1 st each edge of every 4th row 3 (2, 1) time. Inc 1 st each edge of every 6th row 7 (9, 11) times. Work new sts in St st as you inc = 63 (67, 70) sts.

When sleeve measures 11-1/2" (12-1/2", 13-1/2") - 29 (32, 35) cm from beg, bind off all sts.

CHART for Pullover

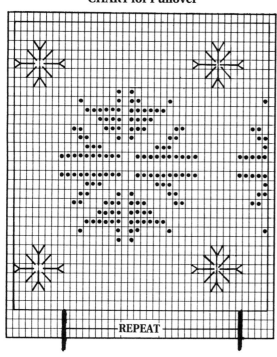

REPEAT

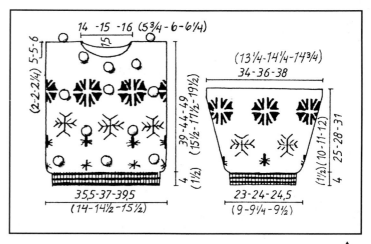

FINISHING: Embroider 4 rows of snowflakes as foll: Row 1: Foll chart 1 in satin st in light blue on either side of the center 17 (19, 21) sts. Beg the embroidery on the 3rd (3rd, 5th) row above the ribbing. Embroider 1 snowflake over the side seams later. Row 2: Embroider small snowflakes by foll chart 2, placing one at each edge of center 15 (17, 19) sts. Beg embroidery on the 19th (23rd, 27th) row above the ribbing. Embroider half snowflake so that center st is next to border st. Row 3: Embroider medium snowflake in light blue, foll chart 3, centering one snowflake and spacing two more, 11 (11, 13) sts apart. Beg embroidery on the 26th (34th, 40th) row above

ribbing. Row 4: Embroider largest snowflakes with blue foll chart 4 at either side of center 5 sts and 2 others spaced 5 sts from the others. Beg the embroidery on the 42nd (52nd, 62nd) row above ribbing. Work 3 rows of snowflakes on the sleeves. Row 1: Embroider the small snowflakes in blue foll chart 2 at center and 2 others spaced 15 (15, 16) sts apart, embroidering to the edges. Beg embroidery on the 6th (8th, 10th) row above ribbing. Row 2: Embroider medium snowflakes foll chart 3 at each edge of center 11 sts. Beg embroidery on the 13th (19th, 23rd) row above ribbing. Row 3: Embroider the largest snowflakes with blue foll chart 4.

Embroider the snowflake in the center, centering chart 4 at M (M ,M1). Embroider snowflakes 5 sts between motifs. Beg on the 30th (38th, 46th) row above ribbing. Sew shoulder seams. With circular needle and blue, pick up and knit 62 (66, 70) sts around neck. Work 1-1/4" (3.5 mm) in 1/1 ribbing as foll: 1 round in blue, 2 rounds in white, 2 rounds in blue, 2 rounds in white, 1 round in blue. Bind off loosely.

Sew sleeves to side seams, matching center of sleeve to shoulder seam. Sew side and sleeve seams. Make 13 pompoms in white 1-1/4" (3 cm) in diameter. Sew on pompoms to front as shown on photo

Snowflake Scarf and Mittens

▼ Materials

Scheepjeswol Superwash Zermatt (50 g) 4 balls White, 1 ball each Blue and Light Blue; U.S. size 4 and 6 (3.5 and 4 mm) knitting needles, U.S. size 4 and 6 (3.5 and 4 mm) double-pointed knitting needles

▼ Gauge

U.S. size 6 (4 mm) needles in St st: 4" (10 cm) = 18 sts x 24 rows.

To save time, take time to check gauge!

▼ Directions

SCARF

With larger size needles and blue, cast on 64 sts and work in St st as foll: 1 row in light blue, 2 rows in white, 2 rows in light blue, 2 rows in white, 2 rows in light blue, continue in white until piece measures 38-1/4" (96 cm) - 220 rows of white. Work 2 rows in light blue, 2 rows in white, 2 rows in light blue, 2 rows in white and 1 row in light blue. Bind off in blue.

FINISHING: Embroider seven large snowflakes foll chart, one above the other along right half of scarf (= first 31 sts after the border st). Beg the embroidery on the 16th row of white after the last light blue stripe. Embroider light blue snowflakes in satin st at each edge of large snowflakes. Embroider first light blue snowflake on the 9th row of white above the last light blue stripe. Fold the scarf right sides tog and sew seam. Turn right side out. Make 8 pompoms in white 1-1/4" (3 cm) in diameter. Sew ends. Sew four pompoms to each end.

MITTENS

With smaller size double pointed needles and light blue, cast on 28 (30, 32) sts and work 1" (1-1/4", 1-1/2") - 2.5 (3, 4) cm in 1/1 ribbing, marking beg of round. Change to larger size double pointed needles and white, work in St st, inc 4 sts on first round = 32 (34, 36) sts. After the 11 (13, 15) round above ribbing: Work 8 (9, 10) sts, place 8 sts on a holder for thumb, cast on 8 sts and work foll 16 (17, 18) sts = 32 (34, 36) sts and continue until piece measures 4-1/2" (5", 6") - 11.5 (13, 15) cm. Dec for top: *sl 1, k1, psso, k12 (13, 14), k2 tog*, rep * to * once. Foll round: *Sl 1, k1, psso, k10 (11, 12), k2 tog* * to * once. Dec in this manner 4 (5, 5) times every round until you have 2 sts between decs. Place rem 8 (6, 8) sts on two needles and knit tog.

THUMB: Pick up 8 sts from holder with light blue and pick up 9 sts from hand. Purl the foll wrong side row and cast on 1 st at end of row. Work 18 sts of thumb for 1-1/4" (1-1/4", 1-1/2") - 3 (3.5, 4) cm. Work the foll row as foll: K1, *sl 1, k1, psso, k4, k2 tog*, rep * to * once,

end with k1. Work 1 row even. Foll row: K1, *sl 1, k1, psso, k2, k2 tog*, rep * to * once, end with k1. Work 1 row even. Break yarn and thread through rem sts. Sew thumb seam.

RIGHT MITTEN: Work same as left mitten. Beg thumb as foll: Work first 16 (17, 18) sts, place 8 sts on holder and cast on 8 sts in their place, work foll 8 (9, 10) sts. Embroider three small snowflakes foll chart for scarf. Place one snowflake at each edge of center 3 (4, 3) sts on the top of hand, beg embroidery on the 5th (6th, 7th) round above ribbing and 1 snowflake on the top of hand beg on the 18th (20th, 22nd) round above ribbing.

CHART 1

CHART 2

CHART 3

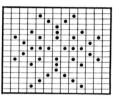

CHART 4

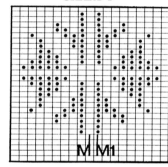

KEY TO CHART

⚫ = Blue

/\ — or | = Light Blue

Zigzag Pullover

▼ Materials

Scheepjeswol Superwash Zermatt (50 g): 3 (4,5) balls White, 2 balls Light Blue, and 2 balls Blue; U.S. size 4 and 6 (3.5 and 4 mm) knitting needles, 16" circular needle U.S. size 4 (3.5 mm)

▼ Gauge

U.S. size 6 (4 mm) needles in St st: 4" (10 cm) = 18 sts x 24 rows.

To save time, take time to check gauge!

▼ Directions

BACK: With smaller size needles and blue, cast on 54 (56, 58) sts and work 1-

1/2" (1-3/4", 2") 4 (4.5, 5) cm in 1/1 ribbing. Purl 1 row on wrong side of work, inc 11 (13, 14) sts evenly spaced across row = 65 (69, 72) sts.

Change to larger size needles, work in St st as foll: 18 (22, 26) rows in blue, 23 rows foll chart 1, beg with 1 border st, point 1 (2, 3), end with point 4 (5, 6), 1 border st, work 16 (20, 24) rows in light blue, 16 rows of chart 2, complete in white. At the same time, when piece measures 9-3/4" (11", 12") - 25 (29, 32) cm from beg, bind off 3 sts at beg of next 2 rows, bind off 2 sts at beg of next 2 rows, dec 1 st at each edge of every 2nd row once = 53 (57, 60) sts. When piece measures 5-3/4" (6-1/4", 6-

1/2") 14.5 (15.5, 16.5) cm from beg of armhole, bind off center 23 (25, 26) sts. Join 2nd ball of yarn to 2nd part and work at the same time. At each neck edge of every 2nd row, bind off 2 sts once. When piece measures measures 6-1/4" (6-1/2", 7") - 16 (17, 18) cm from beg of armhole, bind off rem 13 (14, 15) sts.

FRONT: Beg front same as back, rev charts. When piece measures 4-1/4" (4-3/4", 5") - 11 (12, 13) cm from beg of armhole, bind off center 15 (17, 18) sts. Join 2nd ball of yarn to 2nd part and work at the same time. At each neck edge of every 2nd row, bind off 2 sts twice, dec 1 st twice. Work rem 13 (14, 15) sts on each shoulder. When piece measures 6-1/4" (6-1/2", 7") - 16 (17, 18) cm from beg of armhole, bind off.

SLEEVE: With smaller size needles and white, cast on 32 (34, 34) sts, work 1-1/4" (3.5 cm) in 1/1 ribbing. Purl 1 row on wrong side of work, inc 8(8, 9) sts evenly spaced across row = 40 (42, 43) sts.

Change to larger size needles and white, work in St st. Inc 1 st each edge of every 6th row 6 (7, 7) time. Inc 1 st each edge of every 8th row 2 (2, 3) times. Work new sts in St st as you inc = 56 (60, 63) sts.

When sleeve measures 10-1/2" (11-3/4", 13-") - 27.5 (30.5, 33.5) cm from beg, bind off 4 sts at beg of next 6 rows, bind off 5 (6, 7) sts at beg of next 2 rows. Bind off rem 22 (24, 25) sts.

FINISHING: Sew shoulder seams. With circular needle and white, pick up and knit 72 (76, 78) sts around neck. Work 4" (10 cm) in 1/1 ribbing. Bind off loosely. Fold neckband in half to inside and slip stitch in place.

Set in sleeves, matching center of sleeve to shoulder seam. Sew side and sleeve seams. Make 18 pompoms in white 1-1/4" (3 cm) in diameter. Sew on pompoms to front and sleeves as shown on photo.

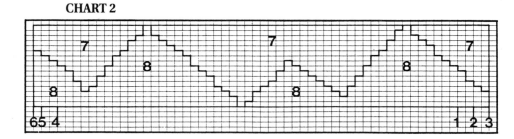

CHART 1

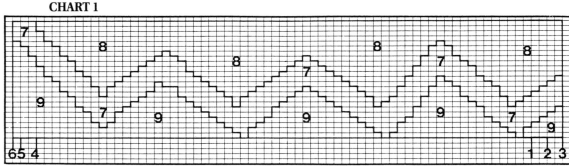

CHART 2

KEY TO CHARTS

7 = White

8 = Light Blue

9 = Blue

Zigzag Scarf and Mittens

▼ Materials

Scheepjeswol Superwash Zermatt (50 g): 2 (3, 3) balls White, and 2 balls each Blue and Light Blue; U.S. size 4 and 6 (3.5 and 4 mm) knitting needles, U.S. size 4 and 6 (3.5 and 4 mm) double-pointed knitting needles

▼ Gauge

U.S. size 6 (4 mm) needles in St st: 4" (10 cm) = 18 sts x 24 rows.

To save time, take time to check gauge!

▼ Directions

SCARF

The scarf is worked back and forth in St st foll charts. Beg and end with 1 border st. Work between points 1 and 2 twice. With larger size needles and white, cast on 66 sts and work in St st as foll: 20 rows in white, 10 rows foll chart 1, *20 rows in light blue, 16 rows of chart 2, 20 rows in blue, 16 rows of chart 3*, work * to * twice total, 20 rows in light blue, 16 rows of chart 2, 20 rows in blue, 10 rows of chart 4, 20 rows in white. When working chart, carry yarn not in use loosely across wrong side of work. Beg and end chart with 1 border st. Bind off.

FINISHING: Block the piece. Fold in half widthwise wrong side together. Sew the long seam. Turn right side out and fold scarf so seam is at one side. Sew ends Make fringe on both ends of scarf. Make 7 strands 2" long. Alternate light blue and blue, spaced 1 st apart. Make a tassel in each corner.

MITTENS

With smaller size double pointed needles and white, cast on 28 (30, 32) sts and work 1" (1-1/4", 1-1/2") - 2.5 (3, 4) cm in 1/1 ribbing, marking beg of round. Change to larger size double pointed needles, work in St st, inc 4 sts on first round = 32 (34, 36) sts. After 6 (8,10) rounds above ribbing, foll chart 5. Work from point 1 (2,3) to point 4 (5,6). Continue in light blue. **At the same time**, after 11 (13,15) rounds above ribbing, work as foll: work 8 (9, 10) sts, place 8 sts on a holder for thumb, cast on 8 sts and work foll 16 (17, 18) sts = 32 (34, 36) sts. Continue in light blue until piece measures 4-1/2" (5", 6") - 11.5 (13, 15) cm, continue in white. Dec for top: *sl 1, k1, psso, k12 (13, 14), k2 tog*, work * to * twice total. Foll round: *Sl 1, k1, psso, k10 (11, 12), k2 tog*, work * to * twice total. Dec in this manner 4 (5, 5) times every row until you have 2 sts between decs. Place

rem 8 (6, 8) sts on two needles and knit tog. Thumb: Work back and forth. Pick up 8 sts from holder with white and pick up 9 sts from hand. Purl the foll wrong side row and cast on 1 st at end of row. Work 18 sts of thumb for 1-1/4" (1-1/4", 1-1/2") - 3 (3.5, 4) cm. end wrong side of work. Work the foll row as foll: K1, *sl 1, k1, psso, k4, k2 tog*, work * to * twice total, end with k1. Purl 1 row. Foll row: K1, *sl 1, k1, psso, k2, k2 tog*, work * to * twice total, end with k1. Purl 1 row. Break yarn and thread through rem sts. Sew thumb seam.

RIGHT MITTEN: Work same as left mitten. Beg thumb as foll: Work first 16 (17, 18) sts, place 8 sts on holder and cast on 8 sts in their place, work foll 8 (9, 10) sts. Make 4 small pompoms with a diameter of 1-1/2" (4 cm). Sew 2 pompoms on the top of the hand on the round above the ribbing spaced 1-1/4" (3 cm) apart.

KEY TO CHART

☐ = White
☒ = Light Blue

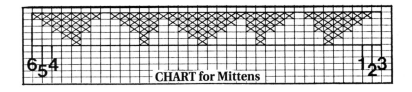

CHART for Mittens

FINISHED MEASUREMENTS

Sizes 2 (3, 4) years -
92 (98, 104) cm

Chest 24-1/4" (26", 27-1/2") -
61 (65, 69) cm

Length 13-1/4" (14", 14-3/4") -
33 (35, 37) cm

Sleeve Length 9-3/4" (10-1/4",
11") - 24.5 (26, 27.5) cm

▼ Materials

Neveda Skol (50 g) 2 (2, 3) balls Blue, 1 (2, 2) balls Red, 1 ball each White and Dark Red; Anchor Embroidery Floss: Gray #0497, Pink #085, Light Pink #023, Light Brown #0426, Peach #0421, Bright Pink #0573, Brown #0428, Black #0403; U.S. size 3 and 4 (3 and 3.5 mm) knitting needles; 4 buttons

▼ Gauge

U.S. size 4 (3.5) needles in St st: 4" (10 cm) = 23 sts x 30 rows.

To save time, take time to check gauge!

▼ Directions

BACK: With smaller size needles and red, cast on 66 (68, 70) sts and work 1-1/2" (4 cm) in 1/1 ribbing. Purl 1 row on wrong side of work, inc 6 (9, 12) sts evenly spaced across row = 72 (77, 82) sts.

Change to larger size needles, work 72 (78, 84) rows in dotted St st by foll chart 2, beg at point 1 (2, 3). Carry unused yarn loosely across wrong side of work. Continue with 6 rows in St st = 78 (84, 90) rows = 11-3/4" (12-3/4", 13-1/2") - 30 (32, 34) cm. Change to smaller size needles and work 1-1/4" (3 cm) in 1/1 ribbing in red. Bind off center 24 (27, 30) sts. Join 2nd ball of yarn to 2nd part and work at the same time. Work rem 24 (25, 26) sts on each shoulder for 1-1/4" (3 cm) in 1/1 ribbing. Bind off.

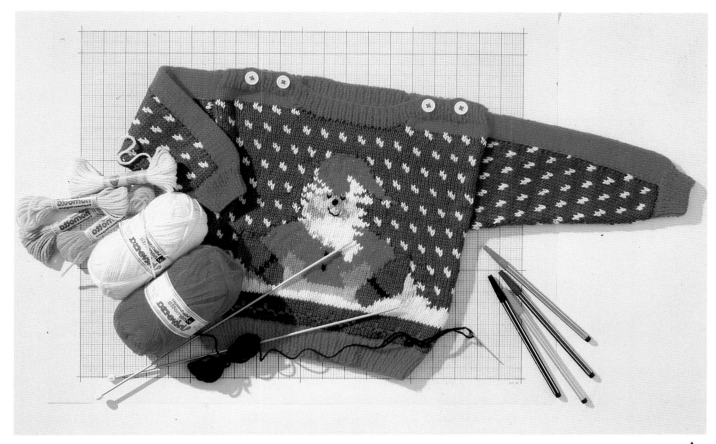

FRONT: Beg front same as back, but after the ribbing work chart 1. Beg with point 1 (2, 3) to point 4 (5, 6). Work in height from point A to B (C, D). Work large motifs (small motifs will be embroidered later). Use a separate ball of yarn for large areas of motif. Be sure to cross yarns on wrong side of work when changing colors. Complete in red. When piece measures 11" (11-3/4", 12-3/4") - 28 (30, 32) cm, place center 16 (19, 22) sts on a holder. Join 2nd ball of yarn to 2nd part and work at the same time. At each neck edge of every 2nd row, place 2 sts on a holder once, place 1 st on a holder twice. Work rem shoulder sts until piece measures 11-3/4" (12-3/4", 13 -1/2") - 30 (32, 34) cm. Work sts on one shoulder, pick up

neck sts on holders, pick up sts from 2nd holder and work in 1/1 ribbing with red. After 1/2" (1.5 cm), make 2 buttonholes on each shoulder as foll: Work 8 (8, 9) sts, bind off 3 sts, work 8 (9, 9) sts, bind off 3 sts, work to last 22 (23, 24) sts, bind off 3 sts, work 8 (9, 9) sts, bind off 3 sts, work 8 (8, 9) sts. On foll row, cast on 3 sts over bound off sts. Work 1-1/4" (3 cm) more in 1/1 ribbing. Bind off. Duplicate stitch small areas on finished work.

SLEEVE: With smaller size needles and red, cast on 32 (34, 34) sts, work 1-1/2" (4 cm) in 1/1 ribbing. Purl 1 row on wrong side of work, inc 9 (9, 10) sts evenly spaced across row = 41 (43, 44) sts.

Change to larger size needles, work in dotted St st as foll: 1 border st, 12 (13, 13) sts in dot pat, 15 (15, 16) sts in red, 12 (13, 13) sts in dot pat, 1 border st. Inc 1 st each edge of every 4th row 12 (13, 14) times. Inc 1 st each edge of every 2nd row 3 times. Work new sts in dot pat as you inc = 71 (75, 78) sts.

When sleeve measures 9-1/2" (10-1/4", 10-3/4") - 24.5 (26, 27.5) cm from beg, bind off all sts.

FINISHING: Embroider the front. Embroider the eyes in black using 2 French knot sts and embroider the mouth in stem st. Overlap the front shoulders over the back and tack ends in place. Sew sleeves to side seams. Sew side and sleeve seams. Sew on buttons.

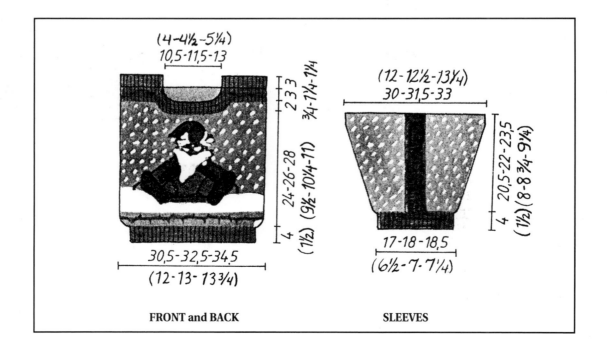

FRONT and BACK   SLEEVES

CHART 1

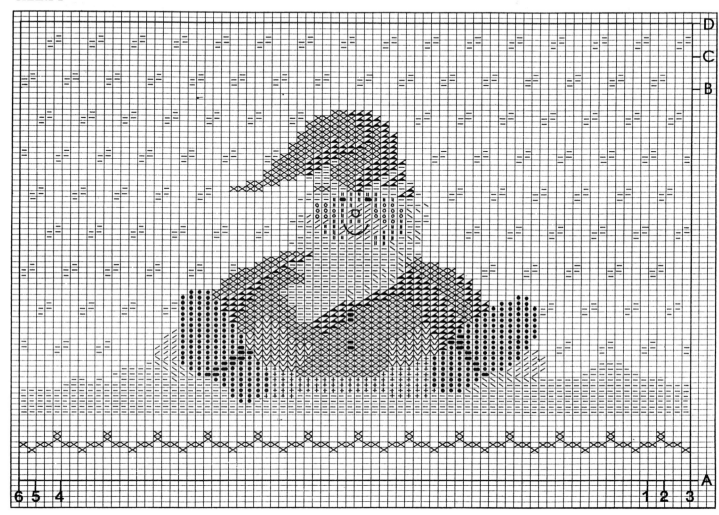

CHART 2

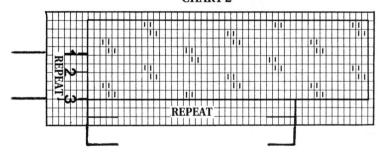

KEY TO CHART

◥ = Gray		☐ = Green	
V = Pink		+ = Bright Pink	
O = Light Pink		X = Red	
‖ = Light Brown		● = Brown	
◢ = Peach		◤ = Dark Red	
– = White		— = Black	

Index

Bibliography

Bredewold, Ank, and Pleiter, Anneke. *The Knitting Design Book.* Asheville, North Carolina: Lark Books, 1988.

Hiatt, June Hemmons. *The Principles of Knitting.* New York City, New York: Simon and Schuster, 1988.

Goldberg, Rhoda Ochser. *The New Knitting Dictionary.* New York City, New York: Crown Publishers, 1984.

The Reader's Digest Complete Guide to Needlework. Pleasantville, New York: The Reader's Digest Association, 1979.

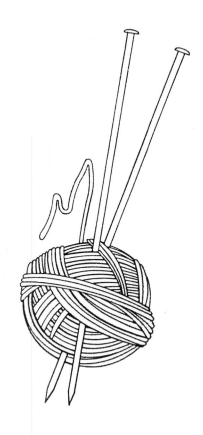

CONVERSION CHART OF KNITTING NEEDLE SIZES														
The needle sizes given in the patterns are recommended starting points for making gauge samples. The needle size actually used should be that on which the stated gauge is obtained.														
United States (US)	0	1	2	3	4	5	6	7	8	9	10	10.5	11	13	15
United Kingdom (UK)	14	13	12	11	10	9	8	7	6	5	4	2	1	00	0000
Metric (MM)	2	2.25	2.75	3	3.25	3.75	4	4.5	5	5.5	6	7	7.5	9	11